ROBERT LONGO

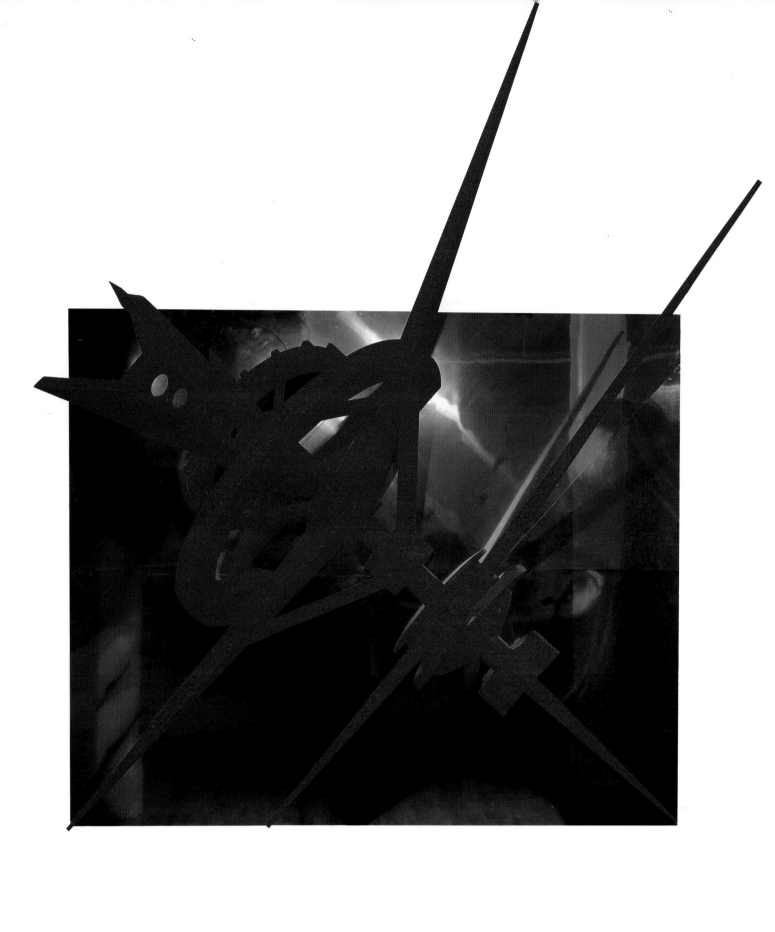

ROBERT LONGO

HOWARD N. FOX

WITH ESSAYS BY HAL FOSTER,
KATHERINE DIECKMANN, BRIAN WALLIS

LOS ANGELES COUNTY MUSEUM OF ART

RIZZOLI, NEW YORK

Published in conjunction with the exhibition
ROBERT LONGO

Los Angeles County Museum of Art
October 1–December 31, 1989

Museum of Contemporary Art, Chicago
February 17–April 22, 1990

Wadsworth Atheneum, Hartford
June 9–September 2, 1990

Designed by Steven Schoenfelder

First published in the United States of America
in 1989 by Rizzoli International Publications, Inc.
300 Park Avenue South, New York, NY 10010

Library of Congress Cataloging-in-Publication Data
Fox, Howard N.
    Robert Longo.
    Includes bibliographical references.
    1. Longo, Robert—Exhibitions.   I. Foster, Hal.
II. Dieckmann, Katherine.   III. Wallis, Brian, 1953–
IV. Los Angeles County Museum of Art.   V. Title.
N6537.L65A4   1989   700'.92   89-45427
ISBN 0-8478-1104-2
ISBN 0-8478-1105-0 (pbk.)

Paul Virilio poem translated by Michel Auder,
Andrew Nuti, and Merrily DeDouhet
Excerpts from J. G. Ballard's Atrocity Exhibition Copyright © 1966,
1970, are reprinted by permission of the author and the
Robin Straus Agency, New York.

Frontispiece: Machines in Love, 1986. See plate 42
Page 6: White Riot I, 1982, unfinished
Page 8: The artist in his studio, 1986

Set in type by Rainsford Type, Danbury, Connecticut,
and David E. Seham Associates, Metuchen, New Jersey
Printed and bound in Japan

CONTENTS

FOREWORD

Since first coming to public attention in the mid-seventies, Robert Longo has created an extraordinary body of work that synthesizes—through drawing, multimedia constructions, video, film, performance, and music—a distinctive artistic expression as unsettling and spectacular as the contemporary world it reflects.

Few artists of the eighties have enjoyed such international visibility as Robert Longo, and few have generated as much thought-provoking commentary about their own art and about the state of contemporary culture at large. Yet even while his highly original art is immediately recognizable by many who have seen only a few examples of it, the fact remains that the works themselves have not, as a whole, been widely exposed. This is, in part, due to the monumental scale and physical complexity of his works, factors that render organizing any exhibition of his art a very difficult challenge, indeed.

Major funding from AT&T, corporate sponsor of this exhibition, has enabled the Los Angeles County Museum of Art to meet this challenge. This presentation brings together for the first time many of the essential works of Robert Longo's creative genius.

The exhibition and its accompanying catalogue trace the formal and thematic development of Longo's art over more than a decade of artistic accomplishment in all the media in which he works. It is our hope in assembling these remarkable works not only to show their stunning visual power as objects but to reveal one of the most penetrating artistic visions of our time, a vision that reflects the deepest anxieties and highest hopes of contemporary civilization.

Earl A. Powell III
Director
Los Angeles County Museum of Art

Sponsor's Statement

For well over a century, AT&T has been in the vanguard of exploring, developing, and forging new links in communications technology.

And for nearly five of those decades, AT&T has been fostering new ideas and ideals in what is perhaps the highest form of communication—the arts.

During all of that time, changes in the arts became as sweeping and profound as those in science and technology. And AT&T has engaged change through its ongoing research and development as well as through its support of human expression in the arts—the current case being this benchmark exhibition of the works of one of America's most provocative artists, Robert Longo.

Perhaps more assertively than any artist of his generation, Longo addresses the experience of living in a world in which instant global communication, the rapid pace of events, and the force of history shape our perception of life and the values we ascribe to it.

This is not the first occasion that AT&T has recognized Robert Longo's compelling vision. In 1984, we prominently featured one of his works in public announcements for an AT&T-sponsored exhibition of contemporary painting and sculpture at The Museum of Modern Art in New York. Now, AT&T marks more than a decade of the artist's distinctive achievement by making possible this presentation of his creative evolution.

R. E. Allen
Chairman of the Board and Chief Executive Officer
AT&T

IN CIVIL WAR

HOWARD N. FOX

Robert Longo has produced some of the most ambitious art being made in the world today. It is ambitious in the finest sense of the word: it has technical virtuosity, in which physical form and content are effectively matched; it has a grandeur of concept, not only addressing contemporary culture but advancing a conviction about art's mission in that culture; and most of all, it projects a vision of human existence in an agnostic age.

Through his art Longo plays out a drama, as old as human culture, of the individual's aspiration for psychological, social, and spiritual fulfillment in life. But this ageless drama takes place in a contemporary culture whose social and political systems often countervail such fulfillment; whose spiritual institutions appear not to address the experience of living in the present age; and whose artistic milieu generally shuns the expression of that aspiration as reactionary, naive, and grossly romantic.

Though Longo's art often involves the human figure, the figures that populate his art are not individuals with personalities and personal histories but function, as Longo says, as "abstract symbols . . . or logos."[1] Indeed, the men and women in his art seem to represent a sort of contemporary Everyman confronting the world. Invested with allegorical significance, Longo's art sustains the concept of the value of human society and the wellbeing of each member of society.

The social commitment revealed in the works is echoed in numerous statements made by Longo throughout the eighties. To begin with, he sees his art as a public, as distinct from a private, activity: "I make art for the public,"[2] he says, squarely setting his practice apart from what may well be the majority of contemporary artists who would assert, as for example Julian Schnabel has, that "my dialogue is with myself, not with exterior forces."[3] Longo, who typically works with many collaborators to produce his art, further asserts: "I'm trying to make work that goes beyond simple private

Fig. 1. Detail of *Seven Seals for Missouri Breaks,* 1976
See plate 1

moments."[4] And in explaining why he chooses not only to create art in forms such as drawing, sculpture, and the mixed-media combine but also to make movies, music videos, performances, and theater spectacles, he says: "I want to produce things that go into our culture quickly."[5]

The themes of cultural engagement and assimilation pervade Longo's art and his outlook. "To be an artist now is not simply to be an isolated being in your studio. It's to have a real serious awareness of all the activities in the world."[6] And he conceives it to be his purpose as an artist to reveal and interpret the values and ideals of contemporary culture and to reflect how we—that is, "the public" Longo addresses—experience that culture and ourselves in it. "I'm totally obsessed with the idea of human value," he has stated, and he believes that "I'm contributing to my culture, posing certain questions about living and the pressures of living today."[7] In fact Longo has deemed the role of the artist to be "the guardian of culture" and considers his function "a responsibility."[8]

Such is the exalted content and expressed moral purpose of Longo's art. And yet it has other, possibly antisocial, aspects, which are hard to articulate but are clearly in evidence, including conflict, rebellion, and envy. The protagonists in Longo's art are repeatedly subjected to control by forces that they and we cannot see; they often appear to fulfill a role that is not of their own choosing but is manipulated or manufactured by cultural forces or social conditions; over and over again, his men and women are caught in the larger machinations of love, war, chaos, and death. And throughout there is a compulsive fascination with—perhaps even an envy of—strength, order, and power.

In its themes and its inspiration, the art of Robert Longo turns on the profound tension between the egoistic demand for autonomy, for power and dominion over all that is not the self, and the equally powerful claims on the individual's allegiance and consciousness by society, politics, and culture, which conspire to determine the self. If there is a central, unifying metaphor in Longo's art it is that of civil war, in which the individual vies for self-governance and authority over the very culture of which he is a member. At the core of Longo's art is an obscure struggle, a dark desire for some forbidden, untenable power, a nearly Faustian quest after a mythical and ultimate freedom. "Power," Longo has reflected, "is the last taboo."[9] That taboo, with its consequences, is his art's heart of darkness.

This mix of exalted elements—the aggrandizement of the individual and the subtext of resistance, the headstrong emotionalism and dark mood of his works and their operatic monumentality—places Longo's art clearly within a romantic tradition that continues

Fig. 2. Study for *Seven Seals for Missouri Breaks,* 1976
Graphite on paper
15 x 18 in. (138 x 46 cm)
Collection Helene Winer, New York

to evolve in today's art, if not always fashionably. Along with such artists as Joseph Beuys, Jonathan Borofsky, Enzo Cucchi, and Anselm Kiefer, Longo perpetuates the romantic tradition and its historical commitment to seeking cultural Truth through individual vision. But although Longo's art has been widely and intelligently discussed, it rarely has been seen in such a fundamentally romantic context. Longo himself has observed: "No critic has ever really romanticized my art; yet *I* think of it as *tragically* romantic."

Indeed, Longo's most admiring writers generally have preferred to focus on the mechanisms of meaning in his art rather than on the meanings themselves. In fact, when his work received its first significant public exposure, in a group exhibition titled *Pictures* (1977), at Artists Space in New York City, guest curator Douglas Crimp, reflecting advanced currents in critical discourse at the time, concentrated in the catalogue not on an interpretation of the art but on the strategy of pictorial representation, identifying "the primary issue in this work [as] . . . the structure of signification."[10] And so, critical discourse on Longo's art has followed in this vein, proposing various models—"re-presentation," allegory, spectacle—for *how* Longo's art

13

means while often circumventing discussion of *what* it means or *may* mean.

Because Longo submits the images from which his art is made to manipulations that, as the critic Craig Owens has contended, "work to empty them of their resonance, their significance, their authoritative claim to meaning,"[11] critics such as Owens have tended to treat the work as opaque and resistant to interpretation—in fact, as an "allegory of unreadability,"[12] suggesting that it is concerned with the very negation of meaning. Brian Wallis has argued that in Longo's performance art, "the forms of the representation are less an interpretation than a system of selection and critical presentation [in which] attention is drawn less to the image itself, the subject matter, than to the process and techniques by which it is formed."[13] Indeed,

Fig. 3. Untitled (Puncher), c. 1978
Graphite and charcoal on paper
31 x 40¾ in. (78.5 x 103.5 cm)
Collection the artist

Fig. 4. Untitled (Cowboy), c. 1978
Graphite and charcoal on paper
31 x 40¼ in. (78.5 x 103.5 cm)
Collection Alyssa Rabach Anthone
and Kenneth D. Anthone,
Buffalo, New York

Jean Fisher has asserted: "The meaning sought [by Longo] is that images intrinsically possess no meaning except that which we impose upon them."[14] Once again, the artist's own statement stands in stark contrast to these analyses: "My work is *about* interpretation. It *forces* interpretation."

If Longo's remark does not necessarily refute those of his commentators, it does reflect a different emphasis. It is thus useful to reexamine his art, now that it has been a publicly visible within the mainstream of American and European art since 1977, and to trace its development with the intent to formulate, rather than to resist, an overall interpretation of the complex meanings at its core.

Like most artists, Longo has made art for as long as he can remember. He recalls that as a child he was always artistically inclined and spent many hours recreating images from movies, television, magazines, and comic books—all the mass media—drawing pictures

of soldiers, cowboys, pilots, and gladiators. Although there is nothing unusual about this—many artists begin to draw early in their lives—in Longo's case it happens that these drawings bespeak an early and abiding fascination with "hero types."

As a high-school student on Long Island, a suburban area near New York City, Longo was active in sports (he was a linebacker on the football team), but he always made time for drawing, sometimes surreptitiously sketching during class. He filled numerous notebooks with his drawings, which often were pictures of soldiers, tanks, football players, astronauts, rock-and-roll musicians, and cowboys. They were rarely individual portraits; instead he made generalized images that he now describes as "archetypes." Longo recalls that he was always amazed at the fascination such images provoked in his fellow students, a fascination he attributes not to his peers' connoisseurship of his draftsmanly abilities but rather to the capacity of familiar images to become emblems of qualities such as action, daring, and energy. Though Longo makes no claims that this had any particular effect on how or what he chose to draw, he recognizes in retrospect that from an early time he was attracted to images that are constructed around culturally codified information.

Like so many artists of his generation, Longo received academic and professional training in the visual arts. After two false starts—first at North Texas State University in Denton, Texas, in 1970, where most of his early course work was in music, and then at Nassau Community College in Garden City, New York—he transferred in 1973 to the State University College at Buffalo, New York, where he graduated in 1975 with a Bachelor of Fine Arts degree. As is sometimes the case with college students, it may be that extracurricular activities were more influential in his development than the academic program. Longo spent many hours in study of the excellent modern

Figs. 5, 6. *Tanks*, c. 1975
Ink on paper
Each, 8 x 10 in.
(22.3 x 25.4 cm)
Collection the artist

15

collections at the Albright-Knox Art Gallery, in Buffalo, and he often describes these experiences as his "real education."

Even more important was his involvement as a cofounder, in 1974, with artists Charles Clough, Nancy Dwyer, Cindy Sherman, and Michael Zwack of the now-legendary Hallwalls, an exhibition and studio space for contemporary art in an old ice factory in Buffalo. Their exhibitions featured significant artists such as Vito Acconci, Robert Irwin, and Jonathan Borofsky; and coordinating these activities gave Longo his first professional involvement with the New York art world as well as his first collaborative experience in the field of art, which would be valuable later in the production of his own work.

Meanwhile, Longo's academic activities were somewhat less sustaining to him. "Art school was lousy,"[15] said Longo of his curriculum at Buffalo, in part because the program did not offer a major in drawing, the one area in which he most wanted to concentrate. Forced to choose, he opted for sculpture because, he reasoned, it was "the closest thing in the college catalogue to a drawing degree."[16] Now the logic of this decision is debatable, but the move itself reveals a certain correlation in Longo's thinking between representation in two- and three-dimensional forms. Moreover, the curriculum shift away from drawing was fortuitous, exposing him more and more to performance, installation, conceptual art, video, and other nontraditional forms, which had become substantial aspects of the school's program in sculpture.

The germinal lesson absorbed by Longo from his academic training—though it is one that would come to full fruition only later on—was that the material and formal properties customarily understood to differentiate two- and three-dimensional media were of much less consequence to his own art than their shared capacity to convey extra-formal content—the culturally codified information implicit in his logolike representations. In fact, he later came to the conviction that transmuting his subject matter from one medium to another, or presenting his subject in radical combinations of media, was "the ultimate test"[17] of his ideas. An early instance of Longo's intermedia transpositions is *Seven Seals for Missouri Breaks* (1976; pl. 1; fig. 1). This painted, cast-aluminum wall relief with its seven incremental images of a rider on horseback emerging from a gorgelike shape is based on a drawing (fig. 2), and this in turn is based on an episode in Arthur Penn's Western movie, *Missouri Breaks* (1976), in which a band of outlaws rides out of a subterranean hiding place. Previously in Longo's development, such a representation might have begun and ended as a drawing; now the work was pointing toward a synthesizing impulse.

However vague that impulse might have been in the artist's imag-

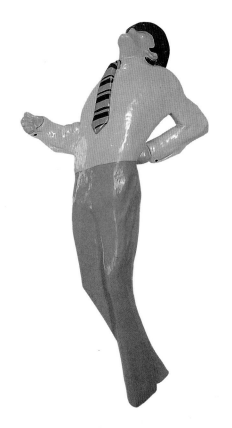

Fig. 7. *The American Soldier,* 1977
See plate 2

16

Fig. 8. Film still from
The American Soldier, 1976
Directed by
Rainer Werner Fassbinder
Courtesy Photofest

ination, it would have a profound effect on his art. In 1977, Longo moved to New York City, dividing his energies among what he saw as the diverse *and separate* activities of making drawings (still of cowboys, sailors, and men on horseback; figs 3–6); frequenting revival movie houses; organizing programs of performance art at The Kitchen Center for Music, Video, and Dance; and hanging out at the punk and New Wave music clubs of downtown Manhattan, where he also played guitar and sang in several rock-and-roll bands. Pulled in so many directions, Longo began to feel the need to synthesize his many interests into a coherent and unified pursuit. "My father used to call me a jack of all trades and a master of none," reflects Longo. "Nothing was enough. I needed to keep adding, to put it all together, to make it be something. I used to destroy things—I loved exploding scale-model cars or setting fire to them. It was crazy. But I'm always putting things together too; *that's* where the creation is."

Longo's impulse to unify his disparate pursuits into a coherent, creative activity—"to make it be something"—found expression in *The American Soldier* (1977; pl. 2; fig. 7), certainly the best known of his transitional works. Its incarnations were much more involuted than those of *Seven Seals for Missouri Breaks* and much more deliberate, ultimately precipitating an entire body of work and manifesting a range of themes that has abided in Longo's art ever since. A painted-aluminum casting, *The American Soldier* depicts the figure of a man wearing a wide-brimmed hat and a striped tie, and he is posed with his torso arched forward and his left hand tucked into the small of his back. Because there is no other information—the silhouetted figure is displayed against the void of a white wall—and no narrative context that explains the figure's suggestive stance, it is impossible

17

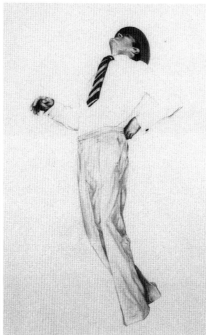

Fig. 9. *Men Trapped in Ice,* 1979
Charcoal and graphite on paper
Three panels, each 60 x 40 in.
(152 x 102 cm)
Courtesy Gagosian Gallery,
New York

to tell what is, or was, or will be happening; the figure could be dying from a knife in the back, or he could be doing the samba. In fact the image was appropriated from a still photograph of the closing scene of Rainer Werner Fassbinder's movie (fig. 8) *The American Soldier* (made in 1970, but released in America in 1976), in which a gangster is shot dead. But in Longo's work the action, or lack of it, remains enigmatic and a source of anxiety for the viewer.

Longo, all but fixated with this uncanny image reflecting an affinity between balletic grace and deadly violence, later used it again and again, subjecting it to much more complex manipulations. It reappeared as a drawing in the center panel of the triptych *Men Trapped in Ice* (1979; fig. 9) and also as a large projected image in a multimedia performance work titled *Sound Distance of a Good Man* (1978; fig. 10), which involved actors, dancers, and musicians performing against a background of projected images. For *Sound Distance,* Longo dressed a friend identically to the figure in Fassbinder's movie in order to restage the cinematic moment. The artist then photographed the restaged moment with a still camera, filmed the resulting still photograph with a motion-picture camera (thereby creating a "nonmotion" motion picture), and projected the static cinema—in which the only action was the flickering light and constantly changing patterns of the film stock's graininess—as a backdrop to the live action of the performance. The image of *The American Soldier* brought together all of Longo's early interests—drawing, sculpture, heroes, popular culture—synthesizing them into a single entity. So seminal was this fusion that in retrospect Longo perceived that many subsequent works, including the entirety of the monumentally scaled Men in the Cities series, "grew directly out of" that single small, painted relief.[18]

All this suggests that if form is not divisible from content in Longo's work, they also are not absolutely one and the same, as modern artists from Kasimir Malevich to Donald Judd had argued they could and ought to be. Longo's transubstantiations of content from one medium to another suggest that his fundamental interests were not

Fig. 10. *Sound Distance of a Good Man*, 1978
In performance at The Kitchen, New York, 1982

focused on material or formal qualities but were more closely preoccupied with signification and meaning in the work; it is very telling that Longo described his works of this period as "misplaced dramas" of "disguised meaningfulness."[19] Indeed, in his transitional works Longo made a deliberate and informed move away from the modernist sensibility, which by the sixties and early seventies had become a largely doctrinaire, critical enterprise devoted to defining the essential nature of art through the primacy of form, material, and process and to promulgating an ideal of the art object's autonomy and independence from the culture at large. Longo's art, with its sources firmly rooted in the culture that it so clearly reflects, had another purpose.

After *The American Soldier*, Longo's misplaced dramas became physically bigger—often with figures lifesize or larger—and emotively more intense. A number of drawings from this period depict young males, singly or in couples, in ambiguous situations that may suggest camaraderie or aloneness or both at the same time. For example, Untitled (Sound Distance of a Good Man) (fig. 11), a 1978 drawing destroyed in a fire, pictures two young men casually standing shoulder to shoulder in a manner that suggests they are buddies. There is no narrative context to indicate why they are together or what they have been doing, but one is buttoning or unbuttoning his shirt, while the other, wearing shirt, tie, and sunglasses, is looking in the opposite direction; though they are intimate in some unspecified way, they are pictured at a moment when each seems isolated in his own thoughts and headed toward a different destiny.

The troubled male bonding of such scenes as Longo was then picturing gives way to combative discord in other works like the 1978 grouping of three aluminum castings, spray-painted with automobile lacquer, titled *The Pilots* (pl. 4), *Swing* (pl. 3), and *The Wrestlers* (pl. 5; fig. 12), in each of which two men are fighting violently with one another. The first two wear gear that identifies them as World War II fighter pilots; the second duo, who look oddly as if they might be dancing with each other, are dressed in contemporary urban garb; the third pair, gripped in an embrace that suggests impassioned lovemaking, are nude; they, too, however, are engaged in combat, and their pose happens to be taken from Pollaiuolo's monumental carving of Hercules and Antaeus (fig. 13).

Though it is hardly possible not to perceive Longo's vision of the manly heroism that unites these classical, yet contemporary, figures, it is quite impossible to discern a coherent narrative. Yet Longo's misplaced dramas convey deep meanings allegorically, if not narratively—that is, they communicate meaning as abstract ideas that are read through the concrete imagery or representation of something else. Unlike narrative, in which meaning is conveyed through a sequence of described events wherein something that happens is followed by something else that happens until a "complete" story is told, in allegory nothing happens.

Allegory, as Craig Owens has described it, is "static, ritualistic, repetitive. It is thus the epitome of counter-narrative, for it arrests narrative in its place."[20] Characteristically, Owens maintains, "al-

legorical imagery is appropriated imagery; the allegorist does not invent images but confiscates them. He lays claim to the culturally significant, poses as its interpreter. And in his hands the image becomes something other (*allos* = other + *agoreuei* = to speak). He does not restore an original meaning that may have been lost or obscured. . . . Rather, he adds another meaning to the image."[21]

Owens's description applies directly to Longo; curiously, Owens finds in his own discussion of Longo that the artist refutes all interpretation through a "blind confrontation of antithetical meanings."[22] This analysis not only undercuts Owens's own premise but also stops far short of the meanings with which Longo has invested his works. Specifically, the works from the late seventies are allegories of male bonding and alienation.

Typically in the works of this period, Longo's coupled protagonists, almost always portrayed as members of the same social or

21

Fig. 12. *The Wrestlers,*
from *Boys Slow Dance,* 1978
See plate 5

Fig. 13. Antonio del Pollaiuolo
Hercules and Antaeus, c. 1460
Bronze
The Bargello, Florence

professional group—fighter pilots of the same squadron, for example—would be expected to share a bond of mutual commitment and purpose; yet they are pitted against one another, hostilely revolting against the bonds of identity and belongingness that unite them. Even when a solitary figure is shown in isolation against a pure white background, as in the image of a man titled *Lone Boy* (1979; fig. 14)—or even in the instances when the figure is a female, such as the young woman in a prom dress (1980; pl. 6)—there is always a violent disruption, a forcible disengagement from the rest of life, as the figure is wrenched from context (the gesture and dress usually imply a distinctly social context) and stopped in mid-action with the jarring quality of a motion picture brought to a dead halt.

A sense of profound disturbance runs through Longo's art like a terrible undertow. Longo's allegories of male bonding and social intercourse are disordered by violence and a determined resistance to social and interpersonal bonds, as well as a refusal to serve their order. This alienation and separateness have a nearly mythic dimension, recalling, perhaps at some subliminal level, Cain's assault against Abel, before which there had not been death, the fall of mankind through disobedience, and the revolt of the Archangel against the ultimate order of Creation. It appears that in Longo's art, or in the creative energy that drives it, opposing psychological forces are at work which inform the disguised meaningfulness at its core.

The full range of Longo's content—heroism, male bonding, social and personal relationships, group identity, the role of the artist in culture, and the underlying violence and refusal to submit to the authority of the group and the culture—came together in his first body of mature work, the series of larger-than-life figure drawings that occasionally were combined with metal reliefs depicting urban architecture, begun in 1979 and collectively titled Men in the Cities. As Longo made more and more works, the protagonists came to look less like movie heroes or literary and advertising images and more like the artist's urban contemporaries, dressed in the uniforms connoting their social identities as young men and women of contemporary urban America. Specifically, the subjects of Men in the Cities are the artist's friends, but they represent a generation of Americans. Longo has referred to the figures in this series as "doomed souls" and "fallen angels."

Like the figure in *The American Soldier*, the images of these men and women are pictures of other pictures; however, they are not appropriated from sources in the mass media but rather from the artist's own photographs produced with numerous collaborators (figs. 15–17). Longo has often compared the process of the Men in the Cities series and subsequent works to motion-picture production and the role to which he aspired in the complex production as a film director. Typically, works from the series began with still photographs created during a shooting session on Longo's roof, in which he costumed his friends and induced their distressed postures and lurching

Fig. 14. *Lone Boy,* 1979
Charcoal and graphite on paper
30½ x 40½ in. (76.2 x 102.8 cm)
Collection Evylyn Wolff-Levy,
New York

23

poses by throwing tennis balls at them or yanking them to and fro with ropes as the camera shutter snapped. Longo then projected the resulting photographs onto large sheets of drawing paper and traced their images in graphite, editing the photographs to delete extraneous information or to change aspects of the figure such as hair style or facial expression. After the fundamentals of each picture were determined, Longo turned over the drawing process to professional illustrator Diane Shea, with whom he has worked since 1979, to flesh out his sketches and fill in the details. Longo then went over Shea's work to make final adjustments. The finished pictures were the result of the collaboration of a team of actors, production assistants, and skilled technicians, with Longo as producer and director.

Figs. 15–17. Three working photographs (originals in color) for Men in the Cities, 1981–87

Figs. 18, 19. Installation views of *Robert Longo: Men in the Cities,* Metro Pictures, New York, 1981

From the outset, Longo envisioned Men in the Cities not as an ongoing project of separate drawings but as a highly structured entirety of stop-motion photographs—not unlike a movie—whose particular elements he combined into distinct groupings and sequences; and when he exhibited them, he always preferred to arrange them so as to suggest a formal and, perhaps, psychological bonding within the sets of figures. For every male figure in Men in the Cities there is a corresponding female, and for every grouping of men there is a counterbalancing group of women (figs. 18, 19). The groupings, always of three or four separate drawings, are determined by the sequence of twisting figures completing the full rotation; although there

are some permutations permitted, Longo's prescribed arrangements are determined systemically.

The groupings are further identified as full, cropped, or reclining—subseries of the whole, which the artist created in that order, as if, over time, these doomed souls were devolving from fully erect figures to fallen ones. And as if to confirm the dramatic structure of this three-year-long series, Longo has commented that to complete the series he finally "killed off" the Men in the Cities with *National Trust* (1981; pl. 25; study, fig. 20), a triptych in which a cast-aluminum relief of a Manhattan skyscraper is flanked by two felled figures, a man and a woman, plainly dead—and, significantly, to-

Fig. 20. Study for *National Trust*,
1981
Charcoal, graphite, and ink on paper
36 x 60 in. (91.5 x 52.4 cm)
Collection Jean Stein, New York

gether for the first time in a single work in Longo's oeuvre. To thus consider Men in the Cities in retrospect and as a unified synthesis of its elements is to behold a misplaced drama, an obscure allegory that suggests both sexuality and human mortality.

But who, it may be asked of these "misplaced dramas," is the protagonist or central dramatic actor? Where does the viewer's attention ultimately fall: on the visual forms, those black-and-white representations *as such*, "freed," as Douglas Crimp has claimed, "from the tyranny of the represented,"[23] or, on the implied subject matter of these representations and on what *does not* appear in them? For although these men and women of the cities stand or fall in stark isolation, wrested from their urban surroundings and plausible contexts, the very theatricality of their unreal circumstances—the allegory in which they perform—trains our attentions, sooner or later, on other dramatis personae not seen on stage.

Carter Ratcliff has suggested that the imaginative focus, if not the visual one, is logically on the central figures who, he says, remind him "of caryatids,"[24] the carved stone figures that functioned as supporting columns in classical architecture, holding up the structure of the most important ceremonial buildings—the very image of humanity upholding its most sacred values. But for Ratcliff, Longo's men and women in the cities are "failed caryatids, wobbling or even crushed . . . [by] the weight of a certain absence that defeats them. They writhe and fall not because their burden is too great but because it is too light—nothing weighs on them, nothing demands their support or offers any to them."[25] In Ratcliff's view, Longo's heroes and heroines are despairing beings, conscious that they are the products of a hollow mass culture of inauthentic values and unreal images; they "twist and collapse under the weight of this vision," realizing that they have "no legitimate burden to bear."[26]

In advancing this reading, Ratcliff appropriately takes on the responsibility of interpreting a body of art that, as the artist asserts, "*forces* interpretation"; and Ratcliff's interpretation, though highly subjective as any reading of Longo's allegories is bound to be, comports with Longo's vision of the protagonists as doomed souls and is rich in speculation on the state of contemporary culture. However, it is precisely because Longo's art *forces* interpretation that any reading which addresses only the condition of the figures represented overlooks the roles of two absolutely essential dramatis personae who happen not to be visually represented: the viewer and the artist. Perhaps more than any other recent artist, Longo forces the viewer's active—even if unwilling—participation in completing, or realizing, the work of art. The strategy itself is nothing new: the Surrealists had exploited the viewer's automatic response to psychologically loaded images; but where the Surrealists' aim was to bypass rational explication of the pictorial images, Longo intentionally provokes a desire for a logical and correct order in his art.

By denying the viewer access to any narrative, yet suggesting that something of profound dramatic consequence has taken place, Longo deliberately tempts—even seduces—the viewer into the pursuit of "ordering" the "unordered" picture. Hardly investigating the structure of signification, Longo's pictures exploit the habitual structure, playing upon the viewer's natural desire to try to figure out what is going on in an unresolved drama. What is most important here is not the particular narrative details that the viewer supplies—"the figures are dancing," or "the figures are dying"—but rather that the viewer has the impulse to supply or conjure up such details. It is the all but instinctual desire of the viewer for explanation, justification, closure, and order—in short, the yearning for an authoritative meaningfulness—upon which the psychological effect and resonance of these works depends.

The dramatic action of these drawings and reliefs thus takes place more in the imagination of the viewer than within the pictures themselves. If Longo's men and women in the cities are dying by bullets, we must ask where the gunfire is coming from, for in these pictures there is no gun and no shootist: "It's not a picture of someone being shot," Longo reminds us; "the person's being shot every time you look at it. . . . You know who the guy is shooting the person: it's you."[27] It is the viewer, asserts Longo, who pulls the trigger.

Thus, against any bidding and without any invitation, Longo preempts the viewer's innocence, aggressively exploiting the viewer's ingenuous response to his visually compelling imagery. And furthermore Longo has confirmed as much in stating that such manipulations had "such incredible hostility for the viewer"[28]—a surprising attitude for an artist who calls himself a guardian of culture and commits his art to the public trust.

It is disingenuous of Longo to shift the blame for an assumed act of violence onto the viewer, for it is the artist, as the works' creator and prime mover, who has engineered the situation in the first place. It is no accident that the Men in the Cities are presented as the *subjects* of forces or events external to them. Their bizarre leaps, twists, recoilings, and falls are strangely devoid of volition or motive: these are instinctual reactions to external forces that they do not control or initiate. Just as he manipulates the viewer, Longo manipulates his own subjects—not only stylistically and formally, as any artist may be said to do, but as an active negotiator of the forces they must hazard to survive. Although Longo's art is rarely autobiographical, he always insinuates himself into his art as an unseen and often hostile force in the condition of his protagonists and as a foil to the viewer. Longo is always an active presence in his misplaced dramas as dramatist and stage manager.

Longo's consistent infringements on the freedom of his figures and his viewers points to his ultimate interest in revealing the larger machinations, the governing powers and forces they obey. His oblique and disguised manhandling of the narratives in his art is geared less at obscuring an event that has taken place than at illuminating a larger system of causation and conditions in which the events are generated. Longo finds less consequence in particulars and events than he does in the systems that perpetrate them, and he employs his art as a metalanguage—as a vocabulary or system of images to disclose the operation of another system.

Indicative of this is his conception of his art as an evolutionary process in which the germinal idea merges with and finally becomes the larger culture. Longo has described the Men in the Cities series, for example, as

a whole system and not just an individual, conscious strategy or gesture based on one particular craft, representation, or style. The [series] expanded and followed itself. . . . As the body of work evolved and began to go through cycles, its scope began to expand; the methods of working grew and became more complicated and more and more people became involved in the making of these works. It moved from drawings, to reliefs, to performances, to combines, to films. . . . As the work was exposed to the public, it was consumed.[29]

Longo has also said that his art follows a clear and necessary "trajectory, leading through art history, film, mass media, and contemporary culture."[30] He intends, always, for his art to transcend the particular, to become the whole.

It was all but inevitable that upon completing the Men in the Cities series Longo would turn from making pictures of individuals to creating revelations of the culture at large. Among the first works to reflect this were several large drawings of typical Men in the Cities figures, but now groups of them, men and women engaged in violent ruckuses, shoving, pulling, and mauling one another. Collectively titled the White Riot series, these friezelike compositions alluded to classical art and its heroic subject matter of real and mythological wars, particularly Michelangelo's relief sculpture *Battle of the Centaurs* (fig. 21). These group pictures culminated in one of Longo's most forceful works of the period, *Corporate Wars: Walls of Influence* (1982; pl. 26; fig. 22), a triptych in whose central cast-aluminum panel some dozen and a half men and women are rendered variously in overhead and straight-on perspective, grappling with one another in a frenzy of possession and escape. This scene of gladiatorial combat, inspired by the artist's observations during a "reconnaissance sortie" to the trading floor of the New York Stock Exchange, is flanked by two massive stylized abstractions of New York's soaring office towers—edifices that Longo recognizes as symbols of consolidated power and its influence over the economy, the political system, and American values generally. In these works, the context of Longo's allegorical art was finally acknowledged.

Even so, these new works shared the fundamental appearance of Men in the Cities as well as the series' now publicly familiar cast of characters and its essential focus. The truly pivotal work at this point in Longo's development, and one that opened up an operatic range of concerns and artistic possibilities, was *Now Everybody* (1982–83; pl. 27). Dedicated to Fassbinder, whose death in June 1982 at the

Fig. 21. Michelangelo Buonarroti
Battle of the Centaurs, c. 1492
Marble
33¼ x 35⅝ in. (84.5 x 90.5 cm)
Casa Buonarroti, Florence

Fig. 22. Center panel of
Corporate Wars: Walls of Influence,
1982
See plate 26

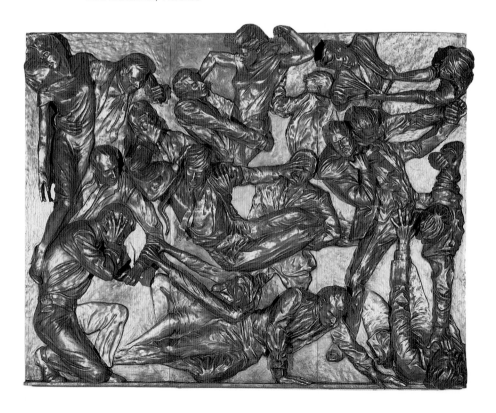

age of thirty-six was felt as a personal loss by Longo, *Now Everybody* featured a lifesize, free-standing bronze sculpture of a shirt-clad, muscular man reeling and pitching forward as if having been shot in the back; behind him, some distance away, is a vast, four-panel drawing, appropriated from a news photograph, of the rubble of Beirut—a city brought to ruin by civil war. For the first time in Longo's work, the figure—the protagonist-victim—has been reunited with the world and the world Longo reveals is in devastation; the image of civilization itself, represented by the city, the tribe, and the culture, has gone hideously awry. (In 1989, Longo created a second version of this work, replacing the image of the Beirut holocaust with a single-panel drawing of a back alley in New York City; the implication of a society in the process of self-destruction is the same.) Typically for Longo, there is no specific narrative, but the relationship of the figure to the background is unmistakable. If this piece lacks the confounding ambiguity of previous works, it vastly magnifies their scope as well as their scale.

In the ensuing combines Longo found his métier. Working on a vast, new scale, with radical combinations of divergent media, such as drawing, photography, and sculpture, and with a palette of materials that might include metal, stone, plastic, and glass in a single work, he discovered the form and expressive mode that matched his impulse to put things—even to force them—into relationship. Whereas the earlier drawings and reliefs had depended on the visual and psychological impact of a single iconic image, the combines make a direct appeal to the imagination with a greatly enriched iconography in a process that Longo has described as replicating the way we experience the contemporary world: through an incessant bombardment of images and information that surrounds us everywhere and penetrates every level of our consciousness. For Longo, those combines represented his preemption of the mass media, his appropriation of their ruthless power and authority for his own ends; and as such, the very technical and formal strategy itself had a political implication for him. Beyond that, the new possibility of total random synthesis into determined order was the essence of his artistic vision.

Though Longo has described the combines in cinematic terms, to be read like storyboards for a movie, it is equally true that they simulate the chronic discontinuity and disjunction of television, mimicking its uncanny juxtapositions of the most incompatible images. Longo keeps a television set on in his studio at virtually all times. Television is, for him, a constant display of popular culture's conceits and an incessant register of the actual happenings and realities of our world. He has described the flow from the video screen—its baffling confluence of cornflake promotions and street murders, its numbing juxtaposition of situation comedies with live coverage of world terrorism—as "the plasma of the culture's vitality." It is video's accelerated tempo and its jarring compression of images and contexts that Longo simulates in the combines.

The combines of the period from 1982 to 1984 are among the most commanding of Longo's epic works, and their exhibition at Metro Pictures in New York in 1984 decisively established him as an artist of international stature. Four of these opuses, *Master Jazz, Pressure, Sword of the Pig*, and *Tongue to the Heart*, are among the most significant works to come out of New York during the intensely vital decade of the eighties. Collectively they encompass the key elements and themes that defined Longo's art at the time.

Master Jazz (1982–83; pl. 30) is an overpowering broadside, nearly twenty feet across, that subjects the viewer to a visual drubbing by means of the most discordant, disturbing images. Each of its four panels represents a fragment in the life of the city; however, the city, it implies, is not a center of human purpose but rather a state of confusion, chaos—an unsynthesized and unordered world. Reading from the left, in the first panel two male urbanites stand shoulder to shoulder but look in opposite directions—a pose echoing that of the two young men in Untitled (Sound Distance of a Good Man) (fig. 11); one of the two appears to be sorely confused. The second panel, a black-lacquered wood relief, depicts the Empire State Building, a symbol of New York City's and America's economic and engineering prowess and optimism; but it is represented as a looming monolith that sucks in all light. In the third panel, an upsetting shift of scale occurs, as the eight-foot-tall face of a black man screams silently into space; Longo has said that the figure was actually a jazz singer, but here he performs either as an aggressor or a victim of some unspoken violence. The final panel depicts a supine white woman, possibly asleep on a bed, possibly dead on the floor.

Throughout, *Master Jazz* beats out a rhythm of tension and portends violence. But possibly the most insidious violence perpetrated in this work is done covertly, by the viewer. The information Longo proffers about his imagined city is, in fact, neutral; and narratively, as is usual in Longo's art, nothing happens. Yet he manipulates the content so that within the viewer there is no celebration of the vitality of the city, no catholic embrace of its myriad populations, and no assent to the lives of its numberless souls. Insidiously, *Master Jazz* breeds the viewer's mistrust, suspicion, and subliminal desire for a more ordered, resolved condition and the authority of certitude. But there is no authoritarian order in Longo's art, only the induced desire in the viewer.

It can be argued that, as far as Longo's protagonists are concerned,

the viewer (and the culture that the viewer represents) is an alien, undermining influence. In *Pressure* (1982–83; pl. 29; fig. 23), one of Longo's most poignant works and among the very few that have a distinct autobiographical inspiration, the viewer plays a sinister role. The troubled central figure, a young man in whiteface traditionally worn by Pierrot, the clown figure in the commedia dell'arte, broods in the lower half of this vertical diptych; bearing down upon him is a massive relief, extending more than three feet into space, of an icy white blockbuster of a building (modeled after the New York Telephone Building in downtown Manhattan), in whose shadow the protagonist sits. His mask, like most costuming in Longo's art, does not serve to cover up an identity but to project one; here, Pierrot's whiteface is used traditionally to symbolize the performer and, by extension, all other artists. The piece is in fact reminiscent of a sculpture Longo had seen nearly ten years before in Paris, Auguste Rodin's *Pallas with the Parthenon* (c. 1896; fig. 24). But now Longo has stated that the protagonist in *Pressure* alludes to himself and that the work was provoked by the anxieties he felt over changes in his life brought about by certain rapid, highly publicized successes in his career and by the pressure to continue to produce significant works.

But in addition to an autobiographical reading of the tension between the public figure and the private self, *Pressure* and related works have other more generalized meanings. Longo's whitefaced protagonist stands for the submissive, obedient individual, perhaps captive or troubled in his role, but ready to assume the values and roles assigned to him by cultural convention. In fact, performing artists appear frequently in Longo's art: a bongo drummer figures in *Body of a Comic* (1984; fig. 25); the singer David Byrne is shown

33

dancing in *Heads Will Roll* (1984; fig. 26); and *Lenny Bleeds: Comet in a Bomber* (1986; pl. 39) is conceived, in part, as a memorial to the comedian and social satirist Lenny Bruce, who died of a drug overdose. In addition, others who must assume a public role—like the astronaut in *Rock for Light* (1983), the soldiers in *We Want God* (1983–84; pl. 34), and the knight in armor in *Still* (1984)—figure prominently in Longo's art of this period.

Significantly, most of Longo's protagonists are passive subjects, performing roles imposed upon them. Even the Everyman figures in the Men in the Cities series are molded by forces external to themselves. All of this suggests that in Longo's art, the performing figure, so iconically represented in *Pressure*, is an allegorical image of vulnerability, of acquiescence, submission, or surrender to cultural roles and conventions and the abdication of the self, always with the viewer's implied complicity.

Though Longo's protagonists are only infrequently combative, the qualities of power and aggression make a vigorous display throughout

Fig. 25. *Body of a Comic,* 1984
Steel drums with motor and timer;
Durotran
120 x 114 x 48 in. (305 x 389.5 x
122 cm)
Collection the artist

34

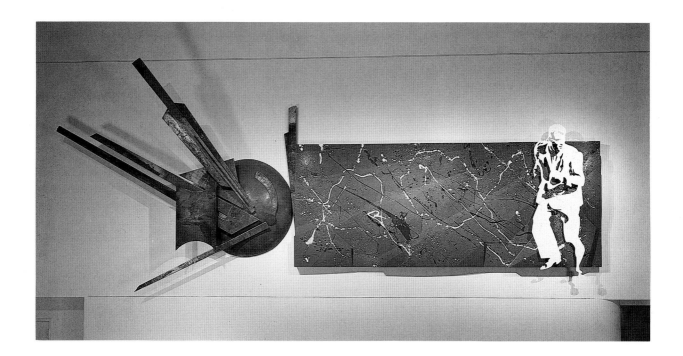

Longo's oeuvre, nowhere more brazenly than in *Sword of the Pig* (1983; pl. 32; study, fig. 27). This expansive triptych, roughly configured like a sword, is emblematic of Western culture's identification of strength with masculinity and of aggression with sexuality. The artist has commented that "the main aim of this piece was basically to make something that was really masculine like a rocket or sword. . . . [It] was a response to being a man in this re-birth of neo-machoism in the culture now."[31] The left panel, which looks like the hilt of a sword, is actually modeled on distortions of the architectural plans of churches, which Longo was then studying.[32] The center panel, influenced by Chaim Soutine's painting *Side of Beef* (c. 1925; fig. 28), is a composite drawing of the grotesquely sinewed bodies of several muscle builders. And the right panel is a silkscreen reproduction of a news photograph of abandoned missile silos in the Midwest.

The clear focus of this work is power and masculinity, but there are far-ranging implications, as well. It is curious but consistent in Longo's art that the least ambiguous works, such as *Now Everybody* (pl. 27), *Sword of the Pig*, and *All You Zombies: Truth before God* (1986; pl. 40) are also the most warlike and savage. In each of these, the cause-and-effect relationship among parts is the most certain, the readings the most explicit. It is as if, for Longo, the very condition of certitude—of authoritative knowledge—is somehow linked to masculinity, aggression, and violence. It is likewise linked to power structures: repeatedly in Longo's art, corporate power, institutional

Fig. 26. *Heads Will Roll*, 1984
Lacquer, oil, and acrylic on wood; epoxy on fiberglass and aluminum
144 x 313 x 46 in. (366 x 795 x 117 cm)
Collection the Eli Broad Family Foundation, Los Angeles

Fig. 27. Study for *Sword of the Pig*, 1983
Charcoal, graphite, ink, and acrylic on paper
30 x 40 in. (76.20 x 101.6 cm)
Collection Jane Holzer and Metro Pictures, New York

Fig. 28. Chaim Soutine
Side of Beef, c. 1925
Oil on canvas
55¼ x 42⅜ in. (140.4 x 107 cm)
Albright-Knox Art Gallery, Buffalo, New York

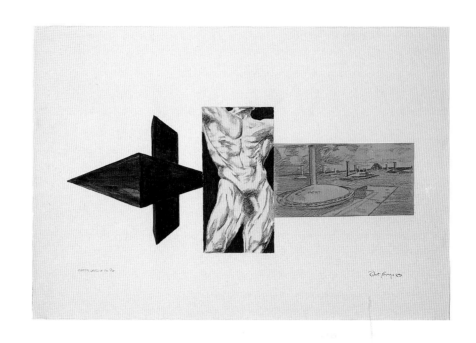

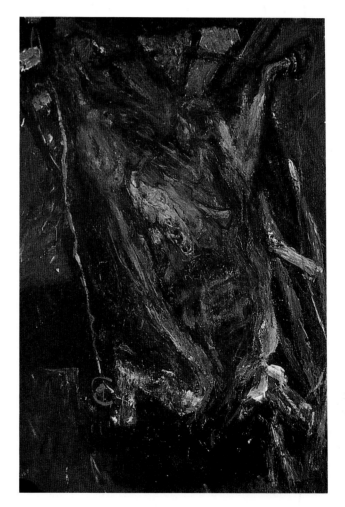

authority (such as the Church, alluded to in the cross-shaped structure in the *Sword of the Pig* or the New York Telephone Building in *Pressure*), and masculine strength are signified by the largest, most severe, and most obvious material forms. Moreover, Longo always represents this strength as hostility and violence; in *Sword of the Pig* it culminates in the threat of total global annihilation. Correlatively, he never portrays strength as a sustaining value or a source of hope in the sense that, say, Christ is conceived as a rock and a redeemer; in Longo's vision, any such rock or redeemer would likely represent specious authority and cultural repression. Perhaps the only hope offered in *Sword of the Pig* is that the missile silos represented are abandoned. Knowing this bit of information enables a reading of the work as signifying the ultimate impotence and sterility of the cultural myth of power; otherwise, *Sword of the Pig* must surely be read as a vision of final self-destruction, an allegorized death wish.

Indeed, a fascination with domination and resistance is a notable aspect of Longo's art in this period. For example, in *Culture Culture* (1982–83; pl. 28), two authorities are set in opposition to one another: a military hero exalted in the form of an equestrian monument is counterposed with a picture of an old man talking on a telephone; the identity of the public hero (Simón Bolívar, actually, memorialized in a statue in New York's Central Park), whose head is not depicted by Longo, is rendered anonymous and irrelevant, while the withered old man (Longo's father, in fact, and therefore something of a private hero to the artist) is made the object of the viewer's curious attention. In *Culture Culture*, the two dissimilar figures are simultaneously heroes and antiheroes, their individual significance a conundrum.

A comparable duality informs *Black Palms* (1983; pl. 33; fig. 29). Like *Pressure*, it is a vertically oriented diptych, its lower section an inverted image of the ruins of a classical civilization (appropriated from Caspar David Friedrich's painting *The Temple of Juno at Agrigentum*, of 1828–30, fig. 30); above it, and seeming to grow out of the ruins, there looms a typically Longoesque skyscraper, its black bulk half soaring, half toppling, and bluntly gouging into the viewer's space. The insinuated conquest of a classical, humanistic civilization by a brutish, monolithic, modern world bodes no good for anybody. In Longo's art, such dualities between private and public, between the historical past and the present, between one authority and another, are locked in futile confrontation, with no clear victor and, always, with dubious spoils.

In its most elemental form, the essential content of Longo's works from 1982 to 1984 can be described as his perception of an unresolved conflict between power and submission, an opposition explored in his masterwork of that period, *Tongue to the Heart* (1984;

Fig. 29. *Black Palms,* 1983
See plate 33

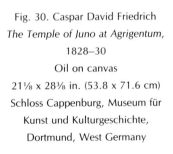

Fig. 30. Caspar David Friedrich
The Temple of Juno at Agrigentum,
1828–30
Oil on canvas
21⅛ x 28⅜ in. (53.8 x 71.6 cm)
Schloss Cappenburg, Museum für
Kunst und Kulturgeschichte,
Dortmund, West Germany

pl. 35). A work of profound vision and lyricality, it is one of Longo's most difficult and unintelligible expressions. The dominant central panel, a relief of hammered lead on wood, depicts a cavernous, vaulted hall that appears to recede deep into space as it towers in height (study, fig. 31). Though it depicts no particular work of extant architecture, its leaden austerity connotes the architecture of Albert Speer, Adolf Hitler's chief architect and urban designer of the Third Reich. It is a structure that insinuates authoritarianism, oppression, and imprisonment; at the same time, it suggests loftiness, grandeur, and idealism. On the left panel, a lifesize plaster cast of a male figure, shown from the torso up, holds his head in his hands, as if

Fig. 31. Study for *Tongue to the Heart,* 1984
Pencil on paper
9 x 12 in. (22.8 x 31 cm)
Collection the artist

he could not bear the sight or sound of something confronting him; he is utterly overwhelmed by whatever it is that he must reckon with. In the right panel, a red mask floats in a void of blackness. In fact, the mask is transparent, revealing a pair of eyes scanning, searching apprehensively, or beholding a vision, but what they see is not disclosed to the viewer. The gaze of wonderment and awe implies an idea of the sublime that is not unlike certain notions of the romantics, expressing the desire to see beyond the threshold of ordinary human knowledge. The three panels, proportioned like an altarpiece, rest above an image of the interminable rolling of the sea.

Everything about *Tongue to the Heart* suggests an infinitude, in which all things merge. Nothing is disordered because nothing is ordered; there is only wholeness. Carter Ratcliff has said that this work is "a monument to incoherence."[33] But it seems more than a celebration of disunity; this grand work represents the search for an all-encompassing order. If *Tongue to the Heart* is not precisely a testament of faith in an ordained universe, it surely is the artist's reflection of man's relentless desire for an ultimate coherence in which all conflict is resolved. *Tongue to the Heart* is nonsectarian and noncredal; it is also as profound and heartfelt a religious work as any in this century.

Like the culture and the myths that they represent, this first group of combines may elicit from the viewer a confused or defensive response. They overwhelm the viewer with arresting images, technical bravura, and daunting size, while proclaiming an urgent meaningfulness to which attention must be paid, even if they do not readily disclose their meaning. Some critics have mistaken Longo's representations of an unresolved universe for a merely unresolved art. Writing of the first exhibition of these combines in 1984, Jean Fisher, for example, complained that in Longo's new body of work "subject matter is ultimately so inconsequential that it becomes primarily 'about' materiality and objectness."[34] Roberta Smith similarly opined: "This is one of the most oppressive art exhibitions I've ever seen. . . . [These works] will stop you in your tracks, but the big question they still raise is: why bother?"[35] And John Howell reflected that for all of Longo's "extravagant conceptual claims, his bombast and sentiment, his epic scale, and his autobiographical insistence," he sometimes produces works that are "so overdetermined, so packed with meaning, that they implode, turning into non sequitur billboards of mystifying—rather than mystical—import." Those images, he went on to say, "don't really resonate—they're just *there*, in a phenomenological muteness that seems at odds with Longo's professed slouching toward meaning."[36]

All such reactions against the disjunctive forms and bullying presence of Longo's art seem to come down to the question of what it means. To reject the work or find it wanting because of its visual discord, its formal "disorganization," and its domineering material presence is precisely to miss its point. Longo's critics are aggravated by the work's hyperactivity and left unsatisfied by its apparent disorder. But they seem to miss the fact that their own desire for resolution and for keeping the work under control is exactly what Longo's art exposes and manipulates. Longo shows us that all of us, himself included, desire an informing order. "Putting things together," as Longo has described it, has always been the sustaining creative impulse in his art.

Thus, the "spiral of fragmentation"[37] that Douglas Crimp sees as the formal basis of Longo's art is just the first half of the equation.

The abortive relationships and discontinuity in Longo's work are but the strategy of signification, not its final resting point. The fulfillment of the equation is much more problematic. Tricia Collins and Richard Millazo are closer to the mark in realizing that discontinuity in Longo's art is "a modernist decoy. What's actually at stake is continuity. . . . Continuity is the false goddess which bestows awareness on our intuitions and instincts. It delivers the lie to our half-moods. It is the line which mediates certitudes of perception and the incertitude of secretly held absolutes."[38]

Indeed, it is not discontinuity and fragmentation but rather the desire for continuity, wholeness, and unity that are the crux of Longo's art. The anxious dilemma dramatized throughout Longo's art, and especially in his works since the mid-eighties, is to distinguish between the individual and society, to determine where the culture stops and the self begins. In Longo's vision the secret absolute is the self, and the infiltration of the culture into the self is a nightmarish perversion.

Several works from a second group of combines of 1985 and 1986 allegorize the vulnerability of the self to the authority of culture and belief systems. Significantly, they feature a menagerie of frightfully deformed monsters and distressed figures penetrated by or joined with alien creatures or things. *Now Is a Creature: The Fly* (1986; pl. 37; study, fig. 32), for example, depicts a pathetically mutated human, crouching on all fours, with skyscrapers sprouting from his back like wings; the work's subtitle alludes to a science-fiction film, also titled *The Fly* (1958), in which a human and a house fly are accidentally merged, resulting in two monstrously deformed figures, one with a human body and a human-size fly's head and the other with a fly's body and a tiny human head. In Longo's work, the science-fiction creature is a metaphor for the individual afflicted malignantly by his milieu.

A comparable hybrid is the sardonic image of *Death and Taxes* (1986; pl. 44), in which a human skull is split by a wedge-shaped avenue of skyscrapers receding into the distance; the clear implication is that the individual may be destroyed—as sure as death and taxes—by the material values of contemporary society. In *Machines in Love* (1986; pl. 42), the image of a man and woman kissing is pierced by the sharp blades of a spacecraft, which dangerously intrudes some five feet into the viewer's space. Here the image of togetherness and intimacy is rendered impotent and turned into an image of separateness by the symbolic interruption of contemporary culture.

Whereas Longo had shown society and culture as burdensome encroachments on the protagonists in earlier works, in the second series of combines these external influences were shown to be vil-

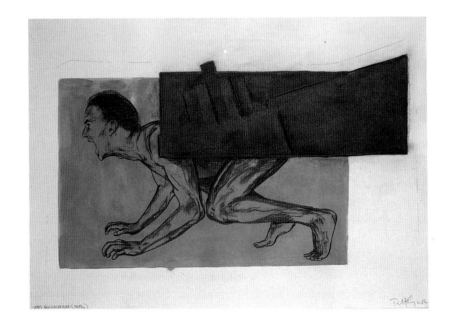

Fig. 32. Study for *Now Is a Creature: The Fly*, 1986
Charcoal, graphite, dye, ink, acrylic dye, and bronze dust on paper
29¾ x 41⅝ in. (75.6 x 105.75 cm)
Collection Edelston/Boardroom
New York

lainous, even aggressively detrimental to the individual. In these works Longo had become preoccupied with the forbidden ideal of the sovereign self—the concept of the individual who is distinct from all other individuals and who is exempt from the strictures and conventions that the culture imposes on all others. As a philosophical concept it is as modern as Friedrich Nietzsche's notion of the *Übermensch*, or Superman; as a mythical construct, it is as ancient as man's first disobedience or, even before that, as the impious war in heaven raised by Satan and his host of rebellious angels. In *All You Zombies: Truth before God* (pl. 40; detail, fig. 33), Longo's most radical and shocking work, the artist reveals the terrible vision of the completely autonomous self.

The monster in *All You Zombies* is a demonic presence roughly in the form of man, yet more like a deformed mass of inchoate, misguided organs and bodily structures. Its helmeted head bears two roaring mouths exposing sharp fangs poised to kill; its scales are pennies, its penis a gun; lightning erupts from its anus; a thousand toy soldiers spill from its disemboweled gut. He is a pathetic demon, as much consumed by his own anger and bodily apparatus as he is aggressive and terrific; yet like so many of Longo's early figures, he seems trapped in ice or fixed in space. And the significance of his aggression is, characteristically for Longo, unresolved: his adversary is neither present nor named, and his defiant brandishing of the sword signals no struggle or victory that can be identified. Indeed, the work stands as an emblem of pure defiance, unqualified by any other purpose or desire.

Longo describes the monster as an image of "American machismo," a confusion of vitality and vigor with warlike destructiveness. Beyond that, this image of individual defiance against external authority is an iconic representation of the secretly held absolute, the "last taboo" of power, autonomy, and authoritarianism. And there is a mythical dimension as well. In *All You Zombies* Longo deliberately evokes the image of the highest angel in eternal rebellion against God, vainly raging for a power he will never attain—the power to control his own destiny. And there is a tragic element implicit in this monster, whose defiance of ultimate authority, like that of Goethe's romantic hero, Dr. Faust, represents the indomitable will to believe in the human spirit, which desires ever more and greater knowledge. The monster is locked forever in civil war with the very power that it envies.

This theme is treated in a less individual, more communal way in the combine *In Civil War* (1986; pl.36). A steel ribbon outlines an abstract, simplified rendering of the map of the United States; stretching across the map, dividing it north and south in a perverse parody of the Mason-Dixon line, is a row of baseball bats hanging pendulous and low. If Longo does not overtly equate the notion of defiant rebellion with the all-American game of baseball, masculine athletic

Fig. 33. Detail of
All You Zombies: Truth before God,
1986
See plate 40

prowess, and male genitalia, he certainly does so subliminally.

In a group of combines from 1988, Longo has raised conflict and tension to a far more ecstatic, abstract state. The perverse monstrosities, descriptive pictorial imagery, and heavily wrought literary conceits have disappeared, to be replaced by a darker, more disciplined vision characterized by hard geometries and terse shapes, a firmly controlled, nearly classical sense of compositional equilibrium, and a distilled, elemental content. Where the dramatic narrative had always been oblique or misplaced in Longo's art, here narrative is sublimated altogether. He has abandoned figures and protagonists, all direct references to time and place, and any reflection of how our culture is presented in the mass media, supplanting them with an iconography that suggests pure forces at work. It is as if he seeks to represent what could be conceived as the "genetic code" of conflict and power.

The theme of civil war persists, but now it is encoded in the most elemental of forms. *A House Divided: Re-enactor* (1988; pl. 48) continues Longo's fascination with the American Civil War and was created after he attended a reenactment of the Battle of Gettysburg on the hundred and twenty-fifth anniversary of that historic event. The imagery of *A House Divided* is little more than a rectangle bisected vertically by a strip of red-painted steel into two panels of blue wool felt, in the color of the Union Army's uniform. Embedded in the surface at dead center of the composition is a polished steel cube. The abstract composition is actually a logolike representation of the Union's uniform, with its blue cloth, red stripes, and silver buttons. But as a single field, split and pierced, seeping a channel of red, it could as well be an iconic representation of any conflict or confrontation of forces.

Similarly iconic in its simplicity is *Black Planet (for A.Z.)* (1988; pl. 51), a grim, foreboding piece dedicated by Longo to his friend and collaborator the performing artist Arnie Zane, who had died of Acquired Immune Deficiency Syndrome. *Black Planet* is the image of a wholeness disrupted, an entity ruptured. Mounted on the wall, a massive spherical section exudes a shock of rubber cables as if spilling out its entrails onto the floor. This herniated world, drained of its potence, is a visual allegory on the loss of power and vitality. There is no victim or actor in it save for the fatal process itself.

Longo continues his absorption with the idea of power in these forbidding works. *Hum: Making Ourselves* (1988; pl. 49) is inspired by the writings of William Gibson, who envisioned the concept of "cyberspace"—describing it as "a consensual hallucination" something like mass hypnosis—in which the universe is imaged as an infinite grid of information where the only stars are dense clusters of data whose terrific power can be accessed by cranial jacks, inputting directly into the brain.[39] In *Hum*, the motif of electronic instrumentation becomes a metaphor for power itself. Like *Pressure*, *Hum* is divided into upper and lower sections. But where *Pressure* depicted a skyscraper in its top half, *Hum* features an abstract form that resembles a giant switchboard or power console. And in place of the whitefaced Pierrot figure in *Pressure's* lower portion, *Hum* bears two polished-steel globes flanking a trunklike sheaf of electrical cables, which erupt from an interior space and splay upward and outward in a profusion of input jacks plugged into the broad field of receptacles above. Longo has commented that the overall form of *Hum* resembles a mask—a motif that appears with some regularity in his oeuvre, as in *Tongue to the Heart* and *Pressure*—and indeed the silver globes faintly suggest a pair of eyes, the grid a head. But the work also has an obvious phallicism in the polished spheres and the thick core of power that bursts out, jacking into the scores of receptacles. It may be that the Pierrot figure has found a revenge for the oppression that haunts him by giving it back to the source; yet *Hum* is plainly a closed system, self-contained and continuous, suggesting an autoerotic orgy of power feeding upon itself.

Dumb Running: The Theory of the Brake (1988; pl. 45; fig. 34) also presents an image of power and force in the form of a machine. It is a simple machine, nothing more than four rows of sleek, gold-leafed cylinders—rollers, actually, like those used to compress red-hot steel into slabs—which appear to hover unsupported directly on the surface of the wall. But they constitute a truly perilous device: the drums spin almost noiselessly and invisibly at terrifically high speed; occasionally, almost at random, they stop, as if halted by a brake—the device that the contemporary French philosopher Paul Virilio, whose writings Longo has studied, has said is the most important invention of the machine age.[40] But, without warning, the cylinders resume their delirious spinning, and the spectator knows instinctually that if he gets too near he runs the risk of being caught and maimed by the machine. The bank of glistening cylinders reels at peak efficiency, with no mission but to be indiscriminately dangerous. For all its brute physical force, *Dumb Running*, like *Tongue to the Heart*, has the distinctly transcendant quality of something surpassing the here and now. *Dumb Running* suggests an absolute power that exists to serve itself and operates on all things external with equal indifference.

In *Joker: Force of Choice* (1988; pl. 46), Longo reintroduces a culturally and emotionally loaded image that he had used previously, the inverted cross. In the earlier work, *End of the Season* (1987; pl. 43), seven steel footballs hang from the cross. In *Joker*, four steel

Fig. 34. Installation view of *Dumb Running: The Theory of the Brake,* 1988,
at Metro Pictures, New York, 1988
See plate 45

wedges are arranged on the wall, forming a negative space that is plainly recognizable as the cross of Christianity, hanging inverted. The inverted cross may suggest a perversion of Christianity itself, or it may recall the crucifixion of St. Peter, who at the time of his martyrdom is said to have asked to be crucified upside down, believing himself unworthy of dying upright. For Longo, the theological interpretation would be extraneous to the image's connotation of depleted strength or failed authority. But the persistent form produced by the hulking steel shapes implies a longing for the cross, which is revealed by its very absence. As happens so frequently in Longo's art, things are discerned in their absence; and what is absent is usually the larger, governing force, which operates like a phantom on that which is visible.

Implicit in Longo's fascination with power, authority, and unity is an attraction to what might be described as fascism and its value of the same things. The artist does not deny an interest in fascism and has gone so far as to comment that it may be at the core of his art, just as it is at the core of contemporary culture: "Fascism isn't just dictatorial regimes, it's a way of thinking. And it doesn't just come in on leather jackets and motorcycles; it comes in on bumperstickers and television. Fascism is our visual culture." But it would be a misunderstanding shared by a number of Longo's observers to conclude that his art "ends up celebrating . . . a political system that can only be repugnant."[41] For it is clear throughout his art that Longo categorically mistrusts public and institutional power. Indeed, in his self-perceived mission as a "guardian of culture," the artist has proved to be far more a militant sentinel against culture's encroachments on the individual than a polemicist or demagogue for any of its particular values or beliefs. Longo's art emphatically does not celebrate totalitarianism.

Longo's art does evoke patterns of thinking that enable a belief in authority and absolute truth; and where these do not exist, true fascism does not exist. Perhaps the deepest confict of all in Longo's art is between his—and our—knowing resistance to fascism, absolutism, and fanaticism and the deeply ingrained cultural desire for knowledge, certitude, order, and power that one recognizes as elements of the positive value of *belief*. Longo's art plays out the central dilemma of postmodern culture, in which belief itself has become a taboo. It is the positive urge to believe that is the first and final motivation of Longo's deeply personal and affecting art. As a "public" artist with a "public" responsibility, Longo never imposes any cultural tenet on the viewer but upholds the value of culture itself in dramatizing the desire, the demand, the compelling necessity to *believe* as a fundamental human drive.

Maurice Berger has suggested that Longo's fascination with power and fascism reflects a cultural malaise, a melancholy "mourning for lost convictions and the hope of new modalities of intellectual belief."[42] Longo himself has echoed this idea, reflecting that "maybe what is heroic is to have a loyalty to things that don't exist anymore, and maybe never did, but you wish they did. Loyalty is a very important thing to have." This is the essential romanticism of Longo's art—it suggests a hope that is at once reasonable and utopian and that is perpetuated in an unrequited desire for shared and abiding values, for individual integrity within the body politic, for the very authority of culture itself.

The questions ultimately posed in Longo's art are political, ethical, and existential. What is the self? What is self-knowledge? What is freedom? These questions are not rhetorical; neither do they pose an answer. But probing their meaning is the fundamental content and creative impulse of his art. In the metaphor of civil war Longo reveals the mute desires, the taboos and anxieties, the cautious doubts and wary beliefs of contemporary culture. From his earliest drawings to his most recent combines, Robert Longo's work bears out his statement that "my art aspires to freedom and truth and hope. It tries to mediate between power and peace."

NOTES

1. Robert Longo quoted by Richard Price in Robert Longo, *Men in the Cities, 1979–1982* (New York: Harry N. Abrams, 1986): 92.

2. Quoted in Carter Ratcliff, "Robert Longo," *Interview* (New York), April 1983: 80.

3. Quoted in Michael Brenson, "Artists Grapple with New Realities," *The New York Times*, 15 May 1983.

4. Quoted in Douglas C. McGill, "Art People: Robert Longo and Collaborators," *The New York Times*, 30 May 1986.

5. Quoted in Paul Gardner, "Longo: Making Art for Brave Eyes," *Artnews* (New York) 84, no. 5 (May 1985): 59.

6. Quoted in Michael Welzenbach, "The Ups and Downs of Art Stardom: An Interview with Robert Longo," *New Art Examiner* (Chicago) 11, no. 4 (December 1984): 42.

7. Quoted in Brenson, 30.

8. Quoted in Ratcliff, 81.

9. All the quotations of the artist not otherwise cited are from conversations with the author between spring 1987 and autumn 1988.

10. Douglas Crimp, catalogue of the exhibition *Pictures*, Artists Space, New York, 1977: 28.

11. Craig Owens, "The Allegorical Impulse: Toward a Theory of Postmodernism, Part 1," *October* (New York), no. 12 (Spring 1980): 69.

12. Craig Owens, "The Allegorical Impulse: Toward a Theory of Postmodernism, Part 2," *October* (New York), no. 13 (Summer 1980): 72.

13. Brian Wallis, "Governing Authority: Robert Longo's Performance 'Empire,'" *Wedge* (New York) 1 (Summer 1982): 64.

14. Jean Fisher, "Reviews: Robert Longo," *Artforum* (New York) 23, no. 1 (September 1984): 116.

15. Quoted in Gardner, 63.

16. Quoted in Longo, 95.

17. Howard N. Fox, "Desire for Pathos: The Art of Robert Longo," *Sun and Moon: A Journal of Literature and Art* (Washington, D.C.) 8 (Fall 1979): 72.

18. Quoted in Longo, 88.

19. Quoted in Fox, 72.

20. Owens, *October*, no. 12, 72.

21. Ibid., 69.

22. Owens, *October*, no. 13, 72.

23. Crimp, *Pictures*, 5.

24. Carter Ratcliff, "Robert Longo: The City of Sheer Image," *The Print Collector's Newsletter* (New York) 14 (July–August 1983): 96.

25. Ibid., 98.

26. Ibid.

27. Quoted in Longo, 101.

28. Ibid.

29. Robert Longo, "Artist's Statement," in catalogue of the exhibition *Robert Longo: Drawings and Reliefs*, Akron Art Museum, Akron, Ohio, 1984: 6.

30. Ibid.

31. Robert Longo, *Talking about "The Sword of the Pig"* (London: The Tate Gallery, Patrons of New Art, 1984): 3, 5.

32. Ibid., 3.

33. Carter Ratcliff, *Robert Longo* (New York: Rizzoli International Publications, 1985): 27.

34. Fisher, 116.

35. Roberta Smith, "Material Concerns," *The Village Voice* (New York), 29 May 1984.

36. John Howell, "Reviews: Robert Longo, The Brooklyn Museum," *Artforum* (New York) 24, no. 2 (October 1985): 120.

37. Douglas Crimp, "Pictures," *October* (New York), no. 8 (Spring 1979): 83.

38. Tricia Collins and Richard Millazo, "Robert Longo: Static Violence," *Flash Art* (Milan), no. 112 (May 1983): 37.

39. William Gibson, *Neuromancer* (New York: Ace Science Fiction Books, 1984): 51.

40. Paul Virilio, in *Pure War*, by Paul Virilio and Sylvere Lotringer, translated by Mark Polizotti (New York: Semiotext, 1984): 45.

41. Sally Banes, "The Long and the Short of It," *The Village Voice* (New York), 18 May 1982: 88.

42. Maurice Berger, catalogue of the exhibition *Endgame: Strategies of Postmodernist Performance*, Hunter College Art Gallery, New York, 1984: 19.

ATROCITY EXHIBITION

HAL FOSTER

It seems to me that his intention is to start World War III, though not, of course, in the usual sense of the term. The blitzkriegs will be fought out on the spinal battlefields, in terms of the postures we assume, of our traumas mimetized in the angle of a wall or balcony.*

More than once Robert Longo has spoken of the artist as a warrior. This is not an allusion to the conventional warfare of the avant-garde: to shock the art public, to transform the art mediums, and so on; the war that concerns Longo has evolved beyond this state. After all, the old military metaphors of the avant-garde presupposed an order to oppose, and though such an order still exists today, it is very difficult to locate. (How, for example, does one *confront* a system as globally diffuse as corporate capitalism, a system that produces disorder as much as order, a system that thrives on its crises as on its successes?) The nonorder of the present is at once so technologically futuristic, politically corrupt, and socially barbaric that the first task of the artist is simply to survive it; the second task is to come to terms with its repertory of images and information; the third is to use these conscious and unconscious representations in order to pressure it; and the fourth is to produce a diagram for change or, in Longoesque terms, an image of a brave new world. It is in this sense that Longo sees the artist as a soldier: part road warrior (à la George Miller), part media scanner (à la David Cronenberg), and part psycho-scientist (à la J. G. Ballard).

For hours they drove through the endless suburbs of the city. The hoardings multiplied around them, walling the streets with giant replicas of napalm bombings in Vietnam, the serial deaths of Elizabeth Taylor and Marilyn Monroe terraced in the landscapes of Dien Bien Phu and the Mekong Delta.

Fig. 1. Detail of *Culture Culture,*
1982–83
See plate 28

---

*The title and italicized passages are from J. G. Ballard's The Atrocity Exhibition *(London: Jonathan Cape, 1970; also published in the United States in 1972 under the title* Love and Napalm*).*

51

Of course Longo is also involved in a more local war—the aesthetic-critical skirmishes of the last ten years. "My generation of artists," he likes to say, "was prematurely rushed to the front"; and yet from his tour of duty Longo has garnered more medals than wounds. At different times his work has served as a privileged example of three of the most important models of postmodernist art: the "pictures" model, according to which art appropriates images that expose the textual nature of representation, for example, the notion that a representation relates to other representations more than to the world; the "allegory" model, according to which art exploits the instability of signification, the gap between an image (signifier) and its meaning (signified); and, finally, the "spectacle" model, according to which art engages our contemporary consumption of reality and history as so many spectacular commodity signs. In its moment each model was persuasive, but in time each has shown its limits.

Using a series of photographs of the most commonplace objects—this office, let us say, a panorama of New York skyscrapers, the naked body of a woman, the face of a catatonic patient—he treated them as if they already were chronograms and extracted the element of time.

In 1977 Douglas Crimp curated the landmark exhibition *Pictures* at Artists Space in New York. Besides Longo, it included Troy Brauntuch, Jack Goldstein, Sherrie Levine, and Philip Smith; in the revised catalogue essay published a year and a half later, Crimp also discussed the work of Cindy Sherman. Five years earlier, in "Other Criteria," Leo Steinberg had used the term "postmodernism" to distinguish the new textual character of contemporary art (his test case was Robert Rauschenberg) from the formalist paradigm of pure painting; in *Pictures* Crimp sought to theorize this difference. The new work could not be measured in terms of style or medium; it cut across too many forms. Rather, it was marked by a new conception of picturing: on the one hand, it contained in tableau form the temporal or theatrical "presence" that modernist-formalist criticism had decried in minimalism and performance (the initiatory work for this generation of artists); on the other hand, it conceived this presence as an effect of representation, its immediacy as a product of mediation. In short, the new art was a conundrum of images: montaged, it advertised its artificiality—it did not pretend to be a representation of the world; appropriated, it advertised its contingency—it did not presume to be an abstraction above the world.

At first sight it seems to be a strange newsreel about the latest tableau sculptures—there are a series of plaster casts of film stars and politicians in bizarre poses—how they were made we can't find out, they seem to have been cast from the living models . . .

The paradigm of these qualities of the artificial and the fragmentary is the film still, which Crimp recognized as the basic device of the new work. This model privileged the Untitled Film Stills of Cindy Sherman in particular, but it also made an image from an early Longo performance, *Sound Distance of a Good Man* (1978; page 19), emblematic of the practice as a whole.

The image shows the upper torso of a man wearing a tie and a hat, his head tilted, his back arched, opposite a statue of a lion; Crimp uncovered its "strata of representation" as follows:

Longo's movie camera was trained on a photograph, or more precisely a photomontage whose separate elements were excerpted from a series of photographs, duplicate versions of the same shot. That shot showed a man dressed and posed in imitation of a sculpted aluminum relief that Longo had exhibited earlier that year. The relief was, in turn, quoted from a newspaper reproduction of a fragment of a film still taken from *The American Soldier*, a film by [Rainer Werner] Fassbinder.

The "scenario" of this film, the scenario just described, the spiral of fragmentation, excerptation, quotation that moves from film still to still film is, of course, absent from the film that the spectators of *Sound Distance of a Good Man* watched. But what, if not that absent scenario, can account for the particular presence of that moving still image?

Such an elaborate manipulation of the image does not really transform it; it fetishizes it. The picture is an object of desire, the desire for the signification that is known to be absent.[1]

Here the work of art is indeed sheer text: an image with no origin except other images; in poststructuralist terms, a signifier in a chain of signifiers along which meaning and desire run. Crimp continues: "Needless to say, we are not in search of sources or origins, but of structures of signification: underneath each picture there is always another picture."[2]

Yet these designs were more than enormous replicas. They were equations that embodied the fundamental relationship between the identity of the film actress, and the millions who were distant reflections of her, and the time and space of their own bodies and postures.

The textuality underscored by Crimp distinguishes postmodernist art from classical modernist art: whereas modernist art "still lays claim to the place and function vacated by religion, still draws its resonance from a conviction that through the work of art some authentic vision of the world is immanently expressed,"[3] postmodernist art uses representation against representation in order to disrupt our naive belief in its referential truth. It is this deconstructive posture that Craig Owens stressed in his 1980 theory of postmodernist art, in which Longo again figured prominently. For Owens, as for Crimp, the crux of postmodernist art is its impulse "to problematize the activity of reference.''[4] Yet according to Owens this impulse leads less to a textual palimpsest of images than to an ambivalent stalemate between readings—the hallmark of the fundamental undecidability of all allegorical representations in which a sign is separated from its meaning. That stalemate for Owens was the pertinence of Longo:

In a recent series of aluminum reliefs, entitled *Boys Slow Dance* and generated from film stills [figs. 2 and 3], Longo presents three images of men locked in . . . deadly combat? amorous embrace? Like [Laurie] Anderson's parables, Longo's images resist ambiguity; they might, in fact, serve as emblems of that blind confrontation of antithetical meanings which characterizes the allegory of unreadability.[5]

Fig. 2. Film still from
Pickup on South Street, 1952
Directed by Samuel Fuller
Courtesy The Museum of Modern
Art, New York
Film Stills Archive

Fig. 3. *Swing,*
from *Boys Slow Dance,* 1978
See plate 3

And, indeed, the early work—including *Seven Seals for Missouri Breaks* (1976; pl. 1), *The American Soldier* (1977; pl. 2), *The Wrestlers* (1978; pl. 5), *The Fall* (1979; fig. 4), and the early Men in the Cities drawings (1979–82)—can be seen in terms not only of the textual model posed by Crimp (neither painting nor sculpture, are these works drawings? reliefs? photographs? photographs of stills? stills of what?) but also of the allegorical model posed by Owens (who are these contorted men and women? do they exist? what are these gestures? do they have a meaning?).

These images of angles and postures constitute not so much a private gallery as a conceptual equation, a fusing device.... In the post-Warhol era a single gesture such as uncrossing one's legs will have more significance than all the pages in War and Peace. In twentieth-century terms the crucifixion, for example, will be re-enacted as a conceptual auto-disaster.

Soon, however, these textual and allegorical models became giv-

Fig. 4. *The Fall*, 1979
Cast hydrostone; lacquer on wood
and steel
96 x 87¾ x 28 in.
(243.7 x 222.8 x 71 cm)
Collection Lannan Foundation,
Los Angeles

ens, as did the device of image appropriation, and Longo treated them as such—conventions to do other things with. It was then that he began obsessively to collide different mediums (in his artwork: drawing, photography, painting, relief, sculpture; in his performances: film, dance, voice, music, image projection). Still, it seemed, this was done in the interest of critique: for why else represent old forms of culture and brazen images of power (as in the Nurembergesque light display in the performance *Empire* or the equestrian statue in the 1982–83 *Culture Culture*) if not to unfasten our fascination with such institutional and/or authoritarian representations? Such considerations prompted, in 1983, the reading of his art in terms of spectacle.[6]

The serene face of the President's widow, painted on clapboard four hundred feet high, moves across the rooftops, disappearing into the haze on the outskirts of the city. There are hundreds of the signs, revealing Jackie in countless familiar postures. Next week there may be an S.S. officer, Beethoven, Christopher Columbus or Fidel Castro.

Longo first focused on spectacle in his 1981 *Empire* performance suite, in which forms of high art and popular culture are taken up, broken down, and reframed. The effect is simultaneously one of enthrallment and estrangement: we become aware of our own seduction, we are exposed to our spectacular consumption of our own alienation. But Longo also manifests a more profound, more problematic engagement with spectacle. On the one hand, his work is an anatomy of spectacle—its erosion of our sense of the real and the historical, its substitution of archaic representations and atavistic feelings. On the other hand, his work is a symptom of the becoming-spectacle of art in general—how aesthetic appearance is more and more governed by the character of the product, how the aura of the artwork is more and more replaced by the fetishism of the commodity. In 1936, Walter Benjamin wrote in "The Work of Art in the Age of Mechanical Reproduction" of the historical passage of art from cult value (art as a ritual instrument) to exhibition value (art as a product for sale). Perhaps now we must speak of the image value of art, of art as a pretext for a spectacular production of commodity signs. For in our time art has assumed the logic of the spectacle—the transformation of objects, events, even people into so many capitalized images—and Longo has at once exposed and advanced this process. Indeed, both the form and the content of his work are dominated by processes of image production and reception. Our "cult of the glossy image," our "death of affect," our "obsession with intensity"[7]—these are among his primary concerns.

Undisturbed now, the vaporizing figures of the dead astronauts diffused across the launching grounds, recreated in the leg stances of a hundred starlets, in a thousand bent auto-fenders, in the million instalment deaths of the serial magazines.

Nevertheless, these Longo productions are counter-spectacles: they work to trick out the fascination effect of spectacular images, to dereify the readymade status of cultural forms. This is why he so aggressively collides old and new styles, mediums, and materials. Take, for example, *Corporate Wars: Walls of Influence* (1982; pl. 26), an aluminum relief of young business people locked in a gladiatorial battle; a mockery of corporate order, it is also a parody of conventional historical representations. Corporate war as a state relief? This is both correct and outrageous, and the effect is at once to expose a present form of power and to explode an ideological medium of history. But such demystification is only a first step for Longo; he now also remythifies his subjects. This operation has several stages. First, he sees in archaic art forms and contemporary media images the figure of history, however kitsched up. Second, he parades these forms and images for our dreamy contemplation. Third, he fragments this "dream-kitsch"[8] in order to open it up to its own contradictions. Thus across an architectural relief Longo juxtaposes a publicity image of a black couple in the surf with a patriotic image of an American astronaut on a spacewalk, as in *Rock for Light* (1983; fig. 5), or beside the figure of a tree he juxtaposes a trench shot of Soviet soldiers in World War II with a portrait of a contemporary American boy, as in *We Want God* (1983–84; pl. 34). The point is not to reconcile these conflicted images on the plane of the marvelous, as in surrealism, nor is it to disprove one image with the other, as in contemporary ideology-critical art; rather, it is to hold them in active suspension, to call out the conflicts, to make the contradictions work, to cancel out the negative charges, and to juice up the positive ones.

As they drove from the town the first hoardings appeared—Cinemascope of breast and thigh, deceit and need...geometry of aggression and desire... diorama of pain and mutilation...elegant declensions of serialized violence ...montaged landscapes of war and death....Travers has at last realized that the real significance of these acts of violence lies elsewhere, in what we might term "the death of affect."

A few examples of each strategy. First there is the canceling of the negative: *Black Palms* (1983; pl. 33) enfolds an abstract black relief of a modern skyscraper on top and an upside-down black painting of a Doric ruin below; almost as radical as the cut in Stanley Kubrick's *2001* (1968) from a bone flung in the air by an ape to a spinning space station, this edit collapses the historical fates of two democracies-become-empires-become-ruins, one ancient, the other contemporary. *Sword of the Pig* (1983; pl. 32) collides a jutting black cross on the left, a red landscape of missile silos on the right, and a yellow torso of a body-builder in the center; the outrageous phallicism of the first image makes it go limp, the excessive buildup of the second saps it; the very overdevelopment of the third attenuates it. Here, virile display—in architecture, society, and world politics—is revealed for the impotent posturing that it is. Second, the juicing up of the positive: in the soldiers of *We Want God* there is a figure of collectivity, however sentimental. So,too, in the black couple of *Rock for Light* there is a figure of social justice, however cooptive, and in the astronaut a figure of new frontiers, however frozen. In short, even the most ideological representations—fascist spectacles, Hollywood films, corporate ads—possess a utopian drive, a collective fantasy that, however corrupt, can be rescued and reused. It is to this end that Longo seizes such ideological images, breaks them up, and then reinscribes them as ciphers of an alternative future. In the most conventional forms of art as in the most destructive forces of society— in *Corporate Wars* and in *Death and Taxes* (1986; pl. 44), in the social blight represented in *Cold Heaven* and in the misbegotten foreign policy suggested in *Dead Reasons* (both 1983–84)—there are lost desires and denied hopes that can be reclaimed and recoded in the interest of a transfigured tomorrow.

Here clock time is no longer valid.... These images are the residues of a remembered moment of time ... warped elements from some placid and harmonious future.

But this practice of image collision might also be obsolescent, for our world of spectacle has begun to fragment of its own accord. This process can be historicized in relation to art in these schematic terms: the logic of capital is to reduce all things and activities to a medium of equivalence for exchange. In the twenties and thirties surrealists countered this logic with a fetishism of archaic objects and serendipitous encounters; theirs was a cultural politics of juxtaposition that worked to resist the passive contemplation of the commodity and to disrupt the spectacular imagescape of the modern city. But it was a battle soon to be lost, for the spectacle became the very cultural order of postwar consumer society. Indeed, in the fifties and sixties the Situationists thought the spectacle could be *détourné* (diverted, appropriated) but not destroyed—its image and events disruptively seized and subversively recoded but never entirely replaced. In a sense, however, they underestimated the (self-) destructive character of capital: in pursuit of profit it will destroy even its own social formations. And, indeed, as Jean Baudrillard and Jonathan Crary have argued, the spectacle has started to implode: for Baudrillard the scene of the spectacle is now mostly displaced by the obscene penetration of all private space, all individual consciousness. And for Crary the televisual-vehicular space of the spectacle is now partly deterritorialized by a new nexus of computer, television, and telephone lines—a nexus that has begun to produce, in conflict with the fetishistically scenic space of the spectacle, a fractured landscape of scattered objects, disjunctive spaces, heterogeneous activities, random investments.

You must understand that for Traven science is the ultimate pornography, analytic activity whose main aim is to isolate objects or events from their contexts in time and space. This obsession with the specific activity of quantified functions is what science shares with pornography. How different from Lautréamont, who brought together the sewing machine and the umbrella on the operating table, identifying the pudenda of the carpet with the woof of the cadaver.

Fig. 5. *Rock for Light*, 1983
Acrylic, charcoal, graphite, and enamel on paper; lacquer on wood; acrylic on aluminum and copper
Three panels, overall 98 x 216 x 36 in. (249 x 549 x 91 cm)
Collection Gerald S. Elliott, Chicago

In this fractured landscape, which the 1970 J. G. Ballard text *Atrocity Exhibition* surveys brilliantly, "sheer contiguity replaces syntax" and "anything can conjoin with anything."[9] It is a landscape that the Western urban subject now inhabits and that the art of Longo now reflects. It is a landscape that explodes not only the surrealist aesthetic of juxtaposition but also perhaps the contemporary practice of image-collision. And, in fact, in works of the last few years Longo has not aggressively collided images, objects, and mediums so much as he has let them arbitrarily conjoin. A work like *Tongue to the Heart* (1984; pl. 35) with its broken synaesthesia of a man with hands over ears, Kafkaesque hall, red gaze in the form of a mask, and silent yellow surf, reads as an epitaph to the spectacle, just as a work like *Still* (1984; fig. 6), with its heart grasped in a hand, nude back, eagle wings, black grid, and armored knight, reads as a random rebus of images ready to be configured at any moment. This hybrid space of events, objects, and signs cannot be mapped, but it can be cut across. And in the recent work, with the possible exception of *Camouflage in Heaven: Swans* (1986; pl. 38), the intersections that result are mostly grim, even deadly—explosively so in the (in) organic intercourse of the spinning satellite and the kissing couple in *Machines in Love* (1986; pl. 42), entropically so in the dim, asocial space of *Lenny Bleeds: Comet in a Bomber* (1986; pl. 39). In effect, this broken world is the dark side of the utopian realm elsewhere projected by Longo, and it is figured demonically in the monster of *All You Zombies: Truth before God* (1986; pl. 40), a horrendous hybrid of the action and horror heroes (a *Predator* born of *Rambo* and *The Terminator*) who dominate the American unconscious.

For him all junctions, whether of our own soft biologies or the hard geometries of these walls and ceilings, are equivalent to one another. What Talbert is searching for is the primary act of intercourse, the first apposition of the dimensions of time and space.

It is, however, in his video and film projects that Longo has most fully explored this new heterotopia of events, objects, and signs. This is made evident in the saturated images and delirious editing of his New Order music video (1986; page 137), and it is made thematic

Fig. 6. *Still*, 1984
Five panels: acrylic and silkscreen on wood; charcoal and graphite on dyed paper; oil and copper leaf on wood; granite and metal; oil on hammered lead
96 x 288 in. (244 x 732 cm)
Collection Edward R. Broida Trust, Los Angeles

in the very narrative of his short film *Arena Brains* (1987; page 140). In this film a schizophrenic figure called The Watcher serves as a screen or relay of six scenes of conflict—between an artist and a critic, among a group of women in a nightclub, among artists at a party, between two would-be thieves, between two affectless lovers, and between an abused woman and an abusive entertainer. In the film The Watcher is indeed a schizo

> open to everything in spite of himself, living in the greatest confusion: He is himself obscene, the obscene prey of the world's obscenity. What characterizes him is less the loss of the real, the light years of estrangement from the real, the pathos of distance and radical separation, as is commonly said: but, very much to the contrary, the absolute proximity, the total instantaneity of things, the feeling of no defense, no retreat. It is the end of interiority and intimacy, the overexposure and transparency of the world which traverses him without obstacle. He can no longer produce the limits of his own being, can no longer play nor stage himself, can no longer produce himself as mirror. He is now only a pure screen, a switching center for all networks of influence.[10]

It is in the war zone between schizoid obscenity and utopian hope that the art of Robert Longo is now to be found.

Fig. 7. Study for *Lenny Bleeds*, 1986
Charcoal, graphite, and acrylic on
paper
18½ x 47½ in. (47 x 120.6 cm)
Collection the artist

NOTES

1. Douglas Crimp, "Pictures." *October* (New York), no. 8 (Spring 1979): 83. Exhibition: September 24–October 29, 1977.

2. Ibid., 87.

3. Fredric Jameson, " 'In the Destructive Element Immerse': Hans-Jurgen Syberberg and Cultural Revolution," *October* (New York), no. 17 (Summer 1981): 111. Jameson here opposes the modernist practice of Syberberg to the postmodernist textuality of Godard.

4. Craig Owens, "The Allegorical Impulse: Toward a Theory of Postmodernism, Part 2," *October* (New York), no. 13 (Summer 1980): 80.

5. Ibid., 72.

6. See my "The Art of Spectacle," *Art in America* (New York) 71, no. 4, (April 1983), and "Contemporary Art and Spectacle," in *Recodings: Art, Spectacle, Cultural Politics* (Port Townsend, Washington: Bay Press, 1985).

7. The first and third phrases are borrowed from Jameson, the second from Ballard.

8. The term is Walter Benjamin's; see Thomas Elsaesser, "Myth as the Phantasmagoria of History: H.J. Syberberg, Cinema and Representation," *New German Critique* 24–25 (Fall–Winter 1981–82).

9. See Jonathan Crary, "The Eclipse of the Spectacle," in *Art after Modernism: Rethinking Representation*, ed. Brian Wallis (Boston and New York: David R. Godine/New Museum, 1984), and "J. G. Ballard and the Promiscuity of Forms," *Zone* 1–2 (1986).

10. Jean Baudrillard, "The Ecstacy of Communication," in *The Anti-Aesthetic: Essays on Postmodern Culture*, ed. Hal Foster (Port Townsend, Washington: Bay Press, 1983): 133.

PLATES

Pl. 1. *Seven Seals for Missouri
Breaks*, 1976
Enamel on cast aluminum
60 x 84 in. (152 x 213 cm)
Collection Maxine and Richard
Brandenburg, Burlington, Vermont 65

Pl. 2. *The American Soldier*, 1977
Enamel on cast aluminum
28 x 16 x 5 in. (71 x 41 x 12.7 cm)
Collection Kasper König, Frankfurt,
West Germany

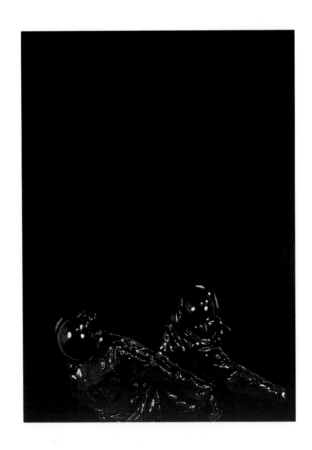

Pls. 3–5. *Triptych: Boys Slow Dance,*
1978

Pl. 3. *Swing,* from *Boys Slow Dance,*
1978
Cast aluminum
21 x 38 x 5 in. (53.3 x 96.5 x 12.7 cm)
Collection Barbara and Oscar
Leidenfrost, Los Angeles

Pl. 4. *The Pilots,* from *Boys Slow
Dance,* 1978
Lacquer on cast aluminum
68 x 49 x 12 in. (172.7 x 124.5 x 32.5 cm)
Collection Marshall and Wallis Katz,
Pittsburgh

Pl. 5. *The Wrestlers,* from *Boys Slow
Dance,* 1978
Lacquer on cast aluminum
40 x 49 x 12 in. (102 x 125 x 30 cm)
Collection Jane Holzer and Metro
Pictures, New York

67

Pl. 6. Untitled, 1980
Charcoal and graphite on paper
45 x 35 in. (114 x 89 cm)
Collection Metro Pictures, New York

Pl. 7. Untitled, 1979
Charcoal and graphite on paper
28 x 40½ in. (71 x 103 cm)
Albright-Knox Art Gallery, Buffalo, New York
James S. Ely Fund, 1980

69

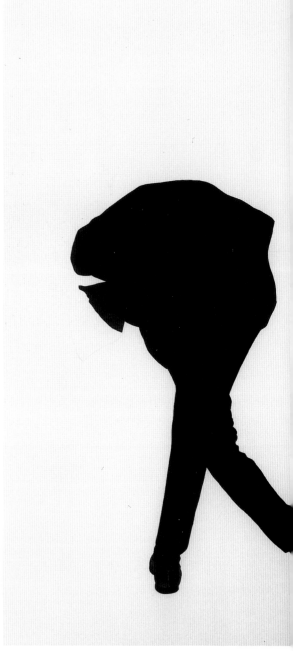

Pl. 8. Untitled, 1980
Charcoal and graphite on paper
Three panels, 36 x 46 in. (91 x 117
cm); 60 x 40 in. (152 x 102 cm); 36
x 46 in. (91 x 117 cm)
Collection Brooke and Carolyn
Alexander, New York

72

Pl. 9. Untitled, 1980
Charcoal and graphite on paper
96 x 60 in. (244 x 152 cm)
Collection Fredrik Roos, Zug,
Switzerland

Pl. 10. Untitled, 1981
Charcoal and graphite on paper
96 x 60 in. (244 x 152 cm)
Collection Metro Pictures, New York

Pl. 11. Untitled, 1981
Charcoal and graphite on paper
96 x 60 in. (244 x 152 cm)
Collection Metro Pictures, New York

Pl. 12. Untitled, 1982–84
Charcoal, graphite, and dye on paper
96 x 60 in. (244 x 152 cm)
Collection the artist

Pl. 13. Untitled, 1981
Charcoal and graphite on paper
96 x 60 in. (244 x 152 cm)
Collection Phoebe Chason,
New York

Pl. 14. Untitled, 1981
Charcoal and graphite on paper
96 x 60 in. (244 x 152 cm)
PaineWebber Group, Inc.,
New York

Pl. 15. Untitled, 1982
Charcoal and graphite on paper
96 x 48 in. (244 x 122 cm)
Collection Mr. and Mrs. Robert K.
Hoffman, Dallas

Pl. 16. Untitled, 1981
Charcoal and graphite on paper
96 x 48 in. (244 x 122 cm)
Collection Arthur and Carol
Goldberg, New York

78

Pl. 17. Untitled, 1982
Charcoal and graphite on paper
96 x 48 in. (244 x 122 cm)
Collection Gerald S. Elliott, Chicago

Pl. 18. Untitled, 1982
Charcoal, graphite, oil, and ink on paper
96 x 48 in. (244 x 122 cm)
Collection Victoria and Albert Killeen,
Atlanta
Not in exhibition

Pl. 19. Untitled, 1981–87
Charcoal, graphite, and ink on paper
96 x 60 in. (244 x 152 cm.)
Courtesy Metro Pictures, New York
Not in Exhibition

Pl. 20. Untitled, 1981–87
Charcoal, graphite, and ink on paper
96 x 60 in. (244 x 152 cm)
Courtesy Metro Pictures, New York
Not in Exhibition

Pl. 21. Untitled, 1981–87
Charcoal, graphite, and ink on paper
96 x 60 in. (244 x 152 cm)
Collection the artist
Not in Exhibition

Opposite: Pl. 22. Untitled, 1981–87
Charcoal, graphite, and ink on paper
96 x 48 in. (244 x 120 cm)
Collection Mr. and Mrs. Robert A.
Krasnow, New York
Not in Exhibition

Opposite: Pl. 23. Untitled, 1982
Charcoal and graphite on paper
60 x 78 in. (152 x 198 cm)
High Museum of Art, Atlanta
Purchased with funds provided by
Edith G. and Philip A. Rhodes and
the National Endowment for the Arts
Not in exhibition

Pl. 24. Untitled, 1981
Charcoal, graphite, ink, and tempera
on paper
96 x 60 in. (244 x 152 cm)
Collection B. Z. and Michael
Schwartz, New York

Pl. 25. *National Trust*, 1981
Charcoal and graphite on paper; cast
aluminum
Three panels, overall 63 x 234 in.
(310 x 594 cm)
Walker Art Center, Minneapolis
Art Center Acquisition Fund, 1981

84

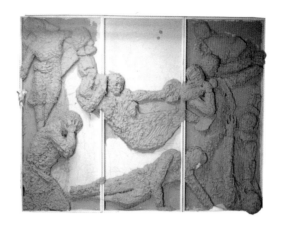

Pl. 26. *Corporate Wars: Walls of
Influence*, 1982
Lacquer on wood and steel; cast aluminum
Three panels, overall 108 x 302 x 48 in.
(274 x 765 x 122 cm)
The Saatchi Collection, London

Top: Model for center panel of
*Corporate Wars: Walls of
Influence*, 1982
Clay

Center panel of *Corporate
Wars: Walls of Influence,* 1982
Cast aluminum

Pl. 27. *Now Everybody (for R. W.
Fassbinder), I.* 1982–83
Charcoal, graphite, and ink on
paper; cast bronze
Four panels, overall 96 x 192 in.
(244 x 488 cm); bronze, 79 x 28 x
45 in. (200 x 71 x 114 cm)
Ludwig Collection, Aachen,
West Germany
Not in exhibition

Pl. 28. *Culture Culture*, 1982–83
Acrylic on Masonite; charcoal,
graphite, oil, acrylic, and ink on paper
with plexiglass
Two panels, overall 91½ x 147¾ in.
(232.5 x 375 cm)
Collection the artist

Pl. 29. *Pressure*, 1982–83
Lacquer on wood; charcoal,
graphite, and ink on paper
Two panels, overall 101½ x 90 x
37¾ in. (258 x 229 x 96 cm)
The Museum of Modern Art,
New York
Gift of the Louis and Bessie Adler
Foundation, Seymour M. Klein,
President, New York

Pl. 30. *Master Jazz*, 1982–83
Lacquer on wood; charcoal,
graphite, and ink on paper;
silkscreen and acrylic on Masonite
Four panels, overall 96 x 225 x
12 in. (244 x 571.5 x 30 cm)
The Menil Collection, Houston

TITLE OF BOOK _____

I bought the book at _____

I received the book as a gift _____

MY COMMENTS: _____
_____
_____

My business or profession _____

Please check off subjects of interest below:

1. ☐ Art
2. ☐ Architecture
3. ☐ Photography
4. ☐ Interior Design
5. ☐ Industrial Design
6. ☐ Graphic Arts

7. ☐ Fashion
8. ☐ Jewelry
9. ☐ Gardens
10. ☐ Judaica
11. ☐ Native American Arts
12. ☐ Travel

13. ☐ Cultural History
14. ☐ Music/Performing Arts
15. ☐ Fiction
16. ☐ Illustrated Gift Books
17. ☐ Nature
18. ☐ Social Science

☐ Yes, please send me the Rizzoli catalog

NAME _____

ADDRESS _____

CITY _____ STATE _____

TELEPHONE NUMBER _____ ZIP CODE _____

All Rizzoli titles are available through your local bookseller.

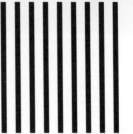

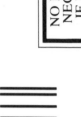

BUSINESS REPLY MAIL

FIRST CLASS PERMIT NO. 1083 NEW YORK, N.Y.

RIZZOLI INTERNATIONAL
PUBLICATIONS, INC.
300 PARK AVENUE SOUTH
NEW YORK, N.Y. 10160–0673

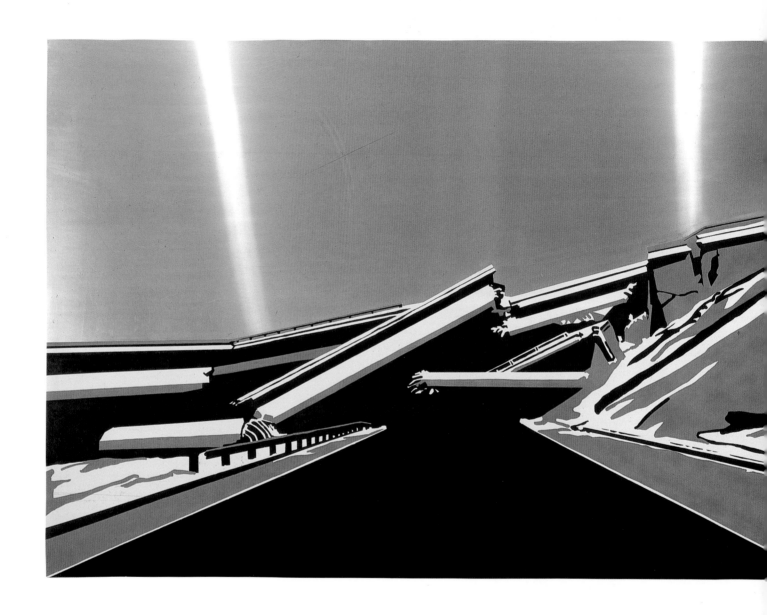

Pl. 31. *Ornamental Love*, 1983
Oil, metal, and linoleum on wood;
charcoal, graphite, and ink on paper;
cast bronze
Three panels, overall 101½ x 202 x
18 in. (258 x 513 x 46 cm)
Collection Janet Green, London

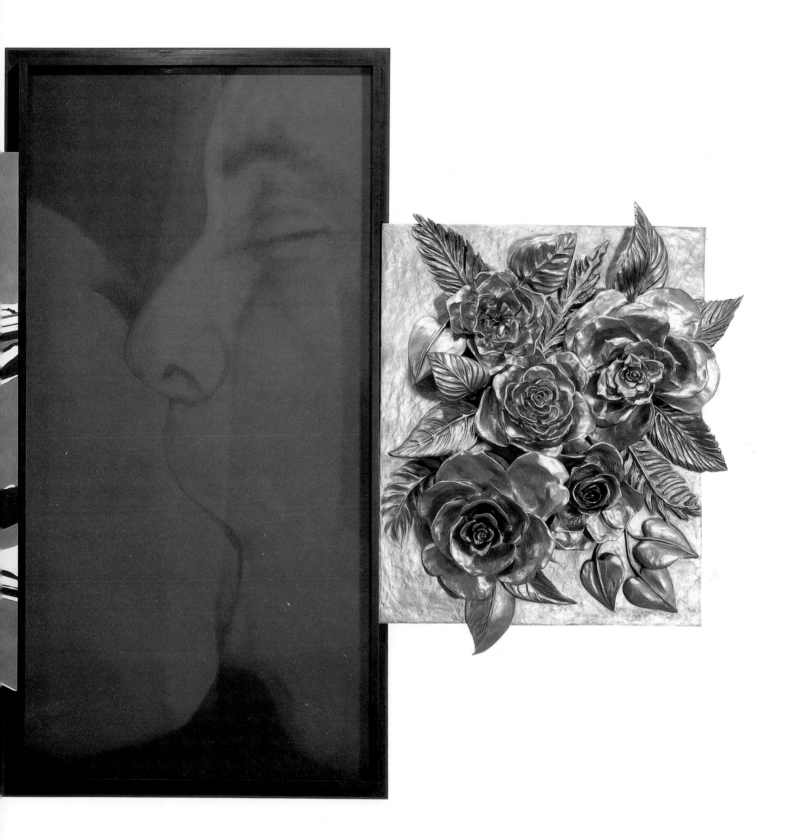

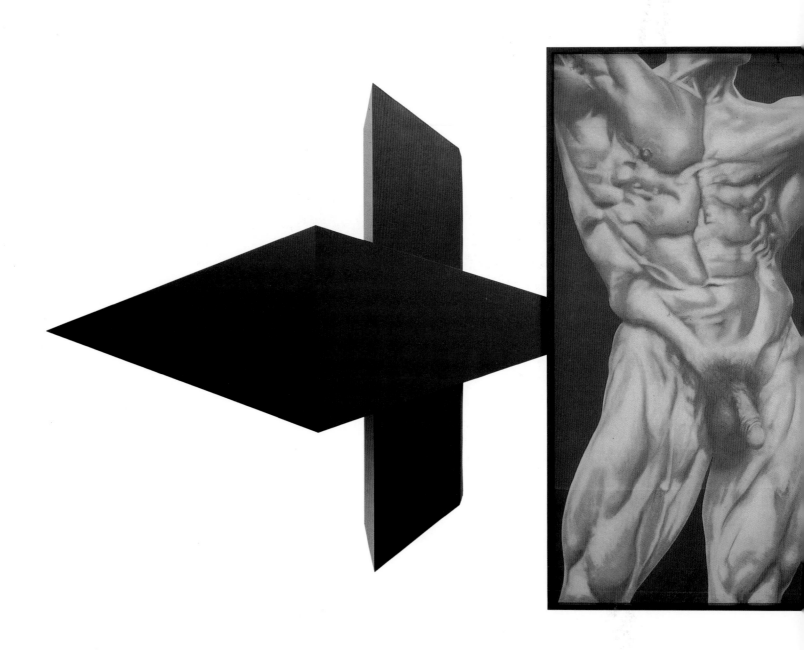

Pl. 32. *Sword of the Pig,* 1983
Lacquer on wood; charcoal and
graphite on paper; plexiglass;
silkscreen on aluminum
Three panels, overall 97¾ x 229½ x
28 in. (248 x 582 x 71 cm)
Tate Gallery, London

Pl. 33. *Black Palms*, 1983
Lacquer, acrylic, and metal on wood
120 x 96 x 29½ in. (305 x 244 x 75 cm)
Collection Mr. and Mrs. C. Bagley
Wright, Seattle

Pl. 34. *We Want God*, 1983–84
Marble; wood; oil on aluminum
Three panels, overall 96 x 115 in.
(244 x 292 cm)
Collection Eugene and Barbara
Schwartz, New York

Pl. 35. *Tongue to the Heart,* 1984
Acrylic and oil on wood; cast plaster;
hammered lead on wood; Durotran;
acrylic, charcoal, and graphite
on canvas
Four panels, overall 136 x 216 x
25 in. (345 x 549 x 63 cm)
The Saatchi Collection, London

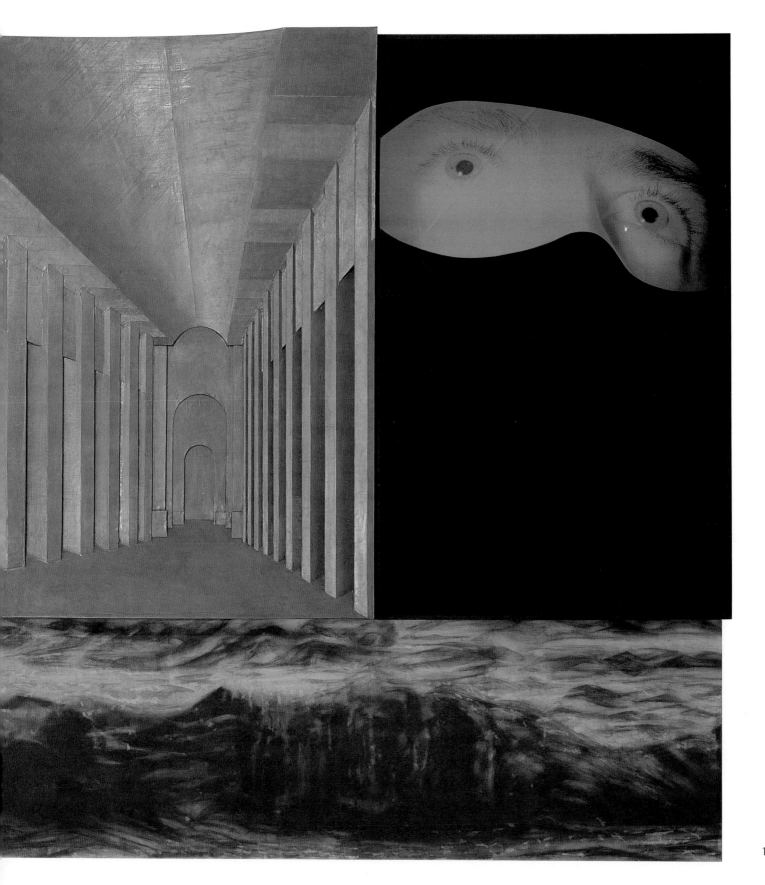

Photograph by Andrew J. Russell,
Battle of Fredericksburg, 1863;
source for background of *In Civil
War*

Pl. 36. *In Civil War,* 1986
Silkscreen on canvas; wood; steel
92¼ x 93 x 5 in. (235 x 236 x 13 cm)
Collection Metro Pictures, New York

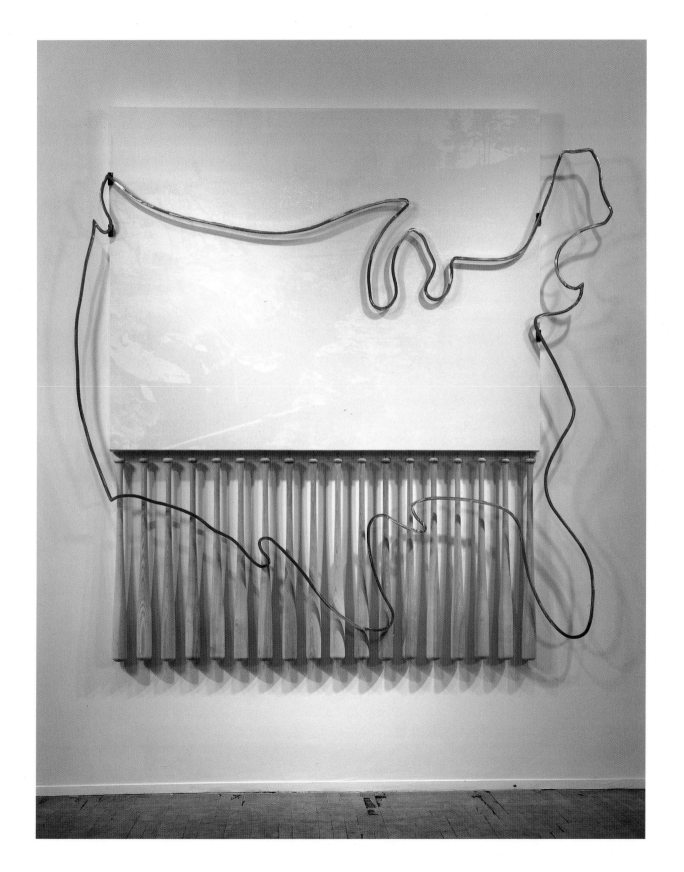

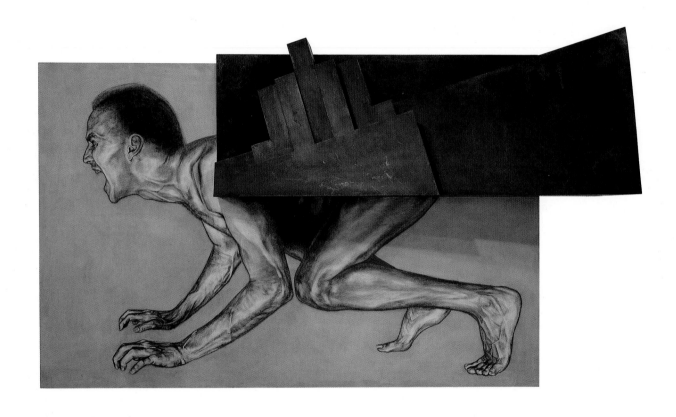

Pl. 37. *Now Is a Creature: The Fly,*
1986
Acrylic, charcoal, and graphite on
canvas; steel
82 x 140 x 26 in. (208 x 355 x 66 cm)
Collection Gerald S. Elliott, Chicago

Pl. 38. *Camouflage in Heaven:*
Swans , 1986
Charcoal, graphite, and acrylic on
canvas; Cor-ten steel and ceramic
tile; chromeplated hydrocal and wood
104 x 321½ x 49½ in. (261 x 816.6 x 126 cm)
Collection William S. Ehrlich,
New York
Not in exhibition

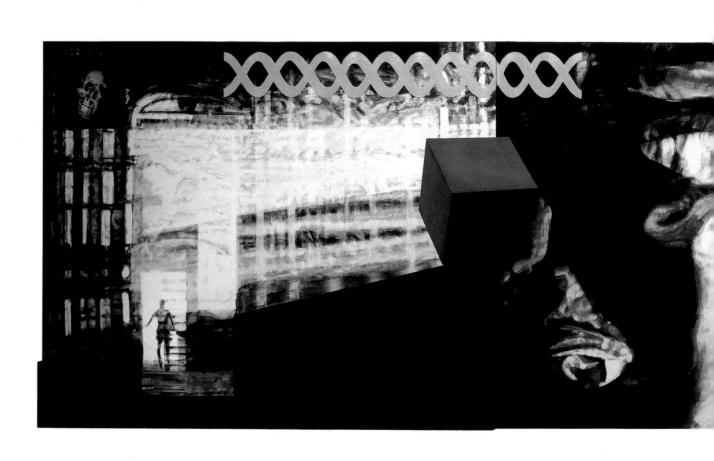

Pl. 39. *Lenny Bleeds: Comet in a
Bomber,* 1986
Acrylic, oil, diamond dust, graphite,
and carbon on canvas; Durotran;
steel; aluminum; and cast bronze
118 x 378 x 39 in. (300 x
960 x 100 cm)
Collection the Eli Broad Family
Foundation, Los Angeles

Pl. 40. *All You Zombies: Truth
before God,* 1986
Acrylic and charcoal on shaped
canvas; cast bronze on motorized
platform of steel and wood
Overall, 176½ x 195 x 177½ in.
(448 x 495.3 x 451 cm)
Collection the artist

Detail of figure, *All You*
Zombies: Truth before God

Pl. 41. *Samurai Overdrive*, 1986
Lacquer on brass; silkscreen on
canvas; lacquer on steel;
plexiglass
126 x 354 x 13 in. (320 x 899 x 33 cm)
Courtesy Metro Pictures, New York
Not in exhibition

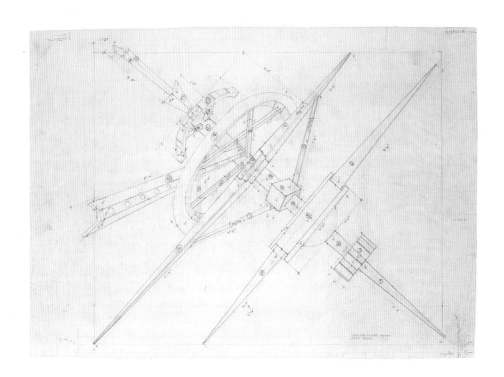

Study for *Machines in Love*, 1986
Graphite on paper
20 x 28¼ in. (51.5 x 71.5 cm)
Collection the artist

Pl. 42. *Machines in Love*, 1986
Silkscreen and enamel on aluminum;
acrylic and oil on wood
Overall, 146 x 133 x 63½ in. (371 x
338 x 161 cm)
Collection Ichizo Ichimura,
Osaka, Japan

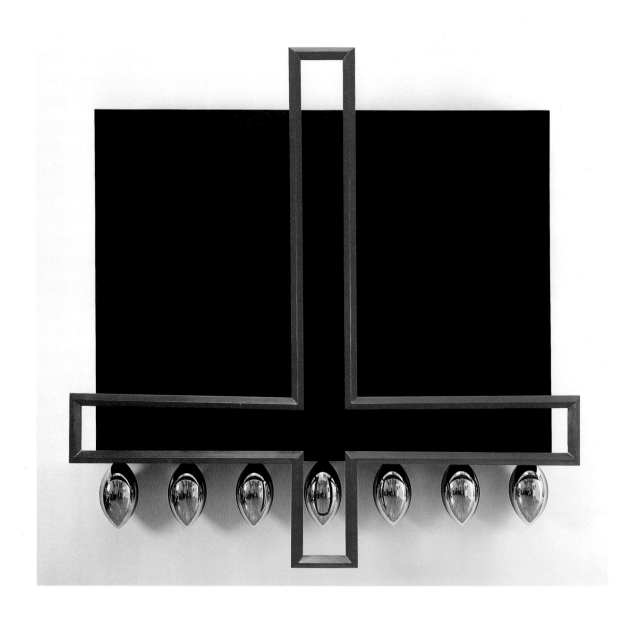

Pl. 43. *End of the Season,* 1987
Linoleum on wood; enamel on steel;
chromeplated cast bronze
96 x 96 x 18 in.
(244 x 244 x 45.8 cm)
Daniel Templon Foundation, Paris

Pl. 44. *Death and Taxes,* 1986
Wood, Cor-ten steel, dollar bills, and
acrylic on wood
Overall, 96 x 92 x 36 in. (244 x 234 x 91 cm)
The Art Institute of Chicago
Restricted gift of Eli Broad Family
Foundation, Mrs. Sandra Crown, Mr.
and Mrs. Thomas Dittmer, Gerald S.
Elliott, David Meitus in memory of A.
James Speyer, Joseph R. Shapiro,
Allen Turner, Kate L. Brewster Fund,
Estate of Louis Lasker Fund, Mrs.
Clive Runnels Fund, and the
Goodman Fund

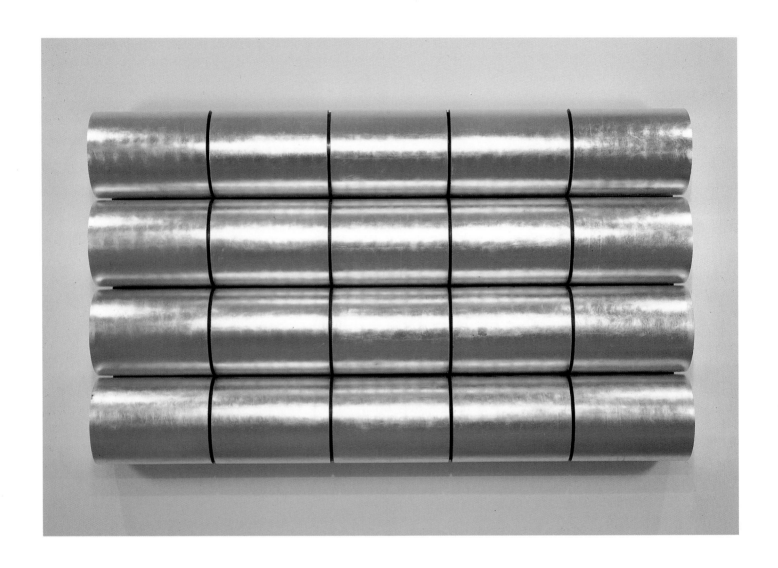

Pl. 45. *Dumb Running: The Theory of the Brake,* 1988
Gold leaf on steel, mounted on recessed steel support, with motor and timer
73 x 126 x 18¾ in. (185 x 320 x 47 cm)
The Langer Collection, New York

Pl. 46. *Joker: Force of Choice,* 1988
Cor-ten steel
Four parts, overall 112½ x 115½ x 18½ in. (286 x 293 x 45.7 cm)
Courtesy Metro Pictures, New York

117

Pl. 47. *Nostromo*, 1986
Patinated copper, wax, felt, lead,
steel, wood, and brick
120 x 159 x 19 in. (304.8 x 403.8 x
48.2 cm)
Collection Fredrik Roos, Zug,
Switzerland
Not in exhibition

Pl. 48. *A House Divided: Re-enactor,*
1988
Wool felt on aluminum; stainless
steel; acrylic paint on aluminum
88 x 126 x 6½ in. (224 x 295 x 16 cm)
Courtesy Metro Pictures, New York

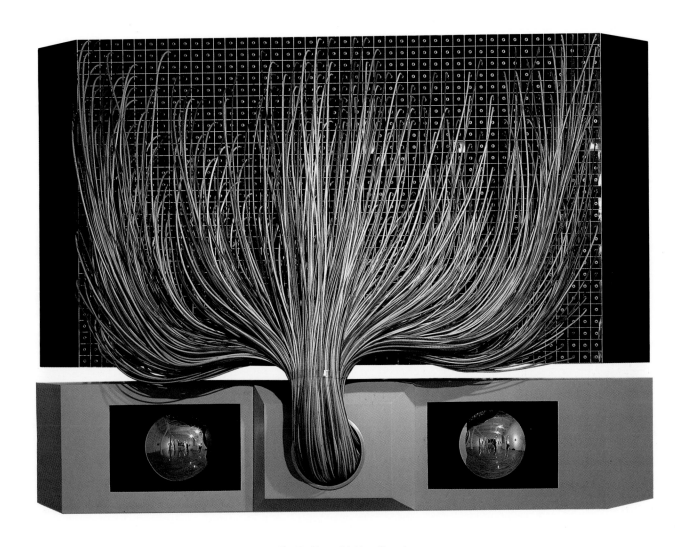

Pl. 49. *Hum: Making Ourselves,*
1988
Formica, plastic tubing, audio jacks,
chromeplated steel, aluminum,
plastic bonding, and lacquer on
wood and steel
Two parts, top 63¾ x 125⅝ x 5⅜ in.
(162 x 319 x 13.7 cm); bottom, 24 x
125⅝ x 28 in. (61 x 319 x 71 cm);
overall 90¾ x 125⅝ x 28 in. (230.5
x 319 x 71 cm)
Collection Barbara and Richard Lane,
New York

Pl. 50. *The Fire Next Time (for
G.B.)*, 1988
Graphite on cast aluminum and
fiberglass; aluminum; plexiglass
74½ x 210½ x 12½ in. (189 x 534 x 32 cm)
The Rivendell Collection

Installation view of *Black Planet*
(for A. Z.), 1988, at Metro Pictures,
New York, 1988

Pl. 51. *Black Planet (for A. Z.)*, 1988
Oil paint on steel; Neoprene
110 x 110 x 72 in. (279 x 279 x 183 cm)
Collection the artist

Small-Screen Stimulus: The Film and Video Work

Katherine Dieckmann

Immersed in a noisy jumble of advertisements, movies, and nightly news broadcasts, Robert Longo collects shards of media imagery and recasts them in his monumental artworks. Serving as both guardian and interpreter of the frenzied late-twentieth-century image bank, his work is a critique on a grand scale. By exaggerating the seductive banality of commercialism—enlarging, reframing, and recontextualizing it—Longo forces his audience to witness the nature of that seduction. His enormous, multipart canvases contain juxtapositions of disconnected pictures (a couple kissing, contorted figures writhing in blank spaces, gilt roses, rubble-strewn urban landscapes, and oppressive and anonymous architectural forms) that jolt us out of a neutralized response to love, violence, and death.

Fig. 1. Still from "Boy (Go)," Golden Palominos, 1986

These confrontational, oversized pieces are also Longo's challenge to art-world conventions. Their sheer mass makes ownership a substantial proposition. A prime example is *All You Zombies: Truth before God* (1986; pl. 40), in which a bronze warrior-victim loaded with symbols of aggression and defeat (a tattered American flag, armor, exhaust pipes, a Magnum revolver) rotates slowly before a curved, painted backdrop of an empty theater. Far too bulky for a living room, this postapocalyptic painting-sculpture is an antiheroic emblem of exhaustion. The mere effort required to move the piece, let alone deduce a clear meaning from it, is a burden.

In 1988, Longo dramatically moved away from media-derived subject matter and created a series of large, abstract wall pieces fabricated from uniform expanses of lead, copper, wax, rubber, or,

127

in the case of *Dumb Running: The Theory of the Brake* (pl. 45), gold leaf. Though somewhat smaller in scale than many of his combines, the new works are just as imposing. These stripped-down, canny revisions of minimalist forms suggest a modernist interest in retrieving the object, tempered with a pervasive skepticism regarding the object's singular strength.

This stripping away of pictures from the solid structures that hold them, as well as a general interest in inflated scale, stems in part from Longo's increasing interest in working as a filmmaker. For the past few years, more and more of his attention has been devoted to the moving image. His most sustained cinematic venture to date is a thirty-four-minute featurette, *Arena Brains* (1987), which satirizes an ambitious New York art world in a series of interwoven sketches. More recently, Longo has developed a feature film based on science-fiction author William Gibson's short story "Johnny Mnemonic," co-scripted by Longo and Victoria Hamburg, which Longo describes as "a thriller set in the near-future about a man with a brain that functions like a computer, and stores secret information that makes people want to kill him. It's like a cross between Godard's *Alphaville* and *The Terminator*."[1] And Longo has been trying for the last decade to launch a full-length feature film called *Steel Angels*—the story of an angry underground comic coming to terms with his vitriolic ways, written by novelist and screenwriter Richard Price.

But Longo has also been rehearsing his new medium in a realm very much outside the gallery circuit and the cinema screen, using a decidedly diminutive frame of reference.

A bastard child of advertising and the record industry, the music video is as short as the average pop song (under five minutes) and is, in some respects, the quintessential eighties commodity. As Gregory Lukow has observed, "More than any previous moving image artifacts, their [music videos'] status as both program and commercial, product and promotion, points to the endless circulation and commodification of moving images in media culture."[2] For Longo, whose work has been described by Hal Foster as "a pretext for the spectacular (re)production of effects, of images, of signs—of sign exchange value,"[3] the music video is the ideal format for condensing pop-culture tropes and exploding them in the viewer's face.

Signature is irrelevant to Music Television and its viewers. The *auteur* behind a video—film directors such as Jonathan Demme, Jim Jarmusch, John Sayles, Brian DePalma, and Bob Rafaelson have made them—is rarely credited publicly. Instead, the work floats amid the twenty-four-hour-a-day whirl of catchy tunes and performers who lip-synch to force feeling into a highly artificial format. Riddled with a repetitive visual lexicon, the medium is ripe for guerilla attack.

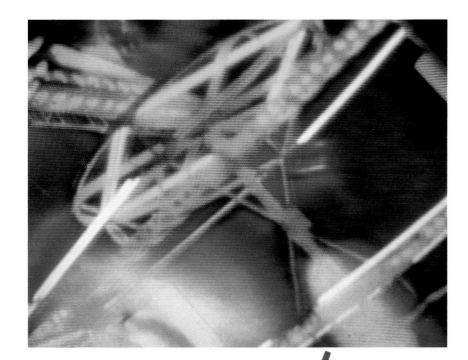

Fig. 2. Still from ''Boy (Go),'' Golden
Palominos, 1986

Fig. 3. *Machines in Love,* 1986
See plate 42

As a response to receiving no on-screen credit for directing music videos, Longo upends the anonymity of the medium with his ironically self-promoting MTV art breaks. The breaks are thirty-second bursts of imagery and text designed to appear between videos and the talking head "veejays" that introduce them. These compressed narratives poke fun at the behavioral patterns induced by watching too much MTV (ignorance of musical history, the mesmerized fogginess of heavy TV viewing). Each concludes with a full-screen-sized "LONGO" blasting across the TV, over-dramatized further by some clanging guitar chords.

While the art breaks are coy interruptions in the narcoleptic flow, it is with Longo's video clips—for the Golden Palominos' "Boy (Go)" (1986), New Order's "Bizarre Love Triangle" (1986), Megadeth's "Peace Sells" (1986), R.E.M.'s "The One I Love" (1987), the World Saxophone Quartet's "Hattie Wall" (1987), Vernon Reid and Living Colour's "Middle Man" (1988), and Rubén Blades's "Hope's on Hold" (1988)—that real revolution can be waged. Here Longo combines his longstanding passion for popular music and cinema to make speedy mini-movies that turn their genre inside out, all the while flirting with becoming just another flash of data in the image bank. The clips are mostly rapidly edited, sometimes to the point of abrasiveness; in Megadeth's "Peace Sells" the strobing climax recalls classic experimental films like Peter Kubelka's *Arnulf Rainer* (1958–60) and Tony Conrad's *Flicker* (1966). But where those films raised perceptual questions in a darkened cinema, Longo's flashes of white light test the viewer's capacity to endure the maximum rapidity and assault that the small screen can unleash.

Such surface frenzy belies the fact that Longo's videos are unusually imaginative, suggesting possible ways of thinking about a song rather than insisting on a literal interpretation of it. They pointedly avoid the genre's facile storytelling and, with the exception of "Hope's on Hold" (Longo's most recent and most conventional clip), forego predictable star-turn performances. With their complex layerings of imagery, bold combinations of live and found footage, mixtures of black-and-white and color, and, particularly in the case of "Boy (Go)" and "Hattie Wall," sophisticated image construction that both adheres to and riffs away from musical rhythms, Longo's clips are more like small experimental movies than works in video. In fact, they are shot on film and then transferred to tape; Longo stresses that "the video is just the box you put the film in."

As a student at the State University College at Buffalo in the mid-seventies, Longo encountered several avant-garde filmmakers at the nearby State University of New York: Hollis Frampton, Michael Snow, Stan Brakhage, Conrad, and Paul Sharits (whom Longo assisted, doing both camera-work and preparatory drawings). Longo was greatly influenced by experimental filmmaking, and his first music video, "Boy (Go)," is in some ways an homage to that visionary tradition, with its emphasis on the evocátive power of the single shot. Exercising the "Kino-Eye" that Dziga Vertov developed in *Man with a Movie Camera* (1928), Longo creates an oppositional montage, blending found and live imagery to present a diffuse (and occasionally nostalgic) picture of natural and machine life—a horse galloping, a jet plane ascending, a ferris wheel spinning, a tree slowly falling, junkyards, and verdant fields, all caught in a swirl of circular movement. While none of these images read as specifically "Longoesque," several of them have inspired later Longo pieces, including *Machines in Love* (1986; pl. 42; fig. 3), which depicts a couple caught in a tight embrace, scarcely visible behind a ferris-wheel-like structure, and *Command* (1986; fig. 5), a drawing of an electric current or lightning bolt—both of which are drawn from image stills in "Boy (Go)" (figs. 2 and 4). This video also reveals Longo's understanding of how editing enhances music: the methodical drumming is emphasized by images such as a pair of black boots walking along a dirt road and the falling chunks of a building, both cut to make the backbeat literal. Thus "Boy (Go)" functions as a curious combination of experimental techniques and a more conventional enhancement of the song being promoted.

In addition to his encounters with nonnarrative filmmakers in his formative years, Longo flirted with video art, the form that was then beginning to supersede film in the vanguard. By the time he moved to New York in 1977, Longo had already experimented with the inexpensive, black-and-white Portapak equipment that inspired video's first wave of artists; he was particularly affected by the work of Vito Acconci, Ed Bowes, Joan Jonas, and William Wegman. They, like most video pioneers, had come to the medium from other disciplines (sculpture, literature, filmmaking), attracted by video's cheapness, accessibility, and potential to initiate McLuhanesque dreams of global communication. As Gregory Battcock points out in his introduction to *New Artists Video* (1978), video was attractive "as a way of introducing advanced ideas that touch upon such subjects as visual perception in communication, criticism and aesthetics, and the potential of new electronic technologies."[4]

Longo has always been interested in technical innovations—as both a means of making art and an image source. Electric sparks, fireworks, a Vandergraf generator, and high-tech computer patterns all appear in his music clips. His first video art pieces were more typical of the dominant idea-oriented strain of the time than glimmers of the forceful combinatorial work to come: studies of water patterns

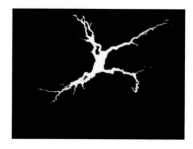

Fig. 4. Still from "Boy (Go)," Golden Palominos, 1986

Fig. 5. *Command*, 1986
Oil and acrylic on canvas; steel; bronze; wood
136½ x 136½ x 14½ in. (346.7 x 346.7 x 35.5 cm)
Courtesy Metro Pictures, New York

in a bathtub, an enigmatic tape of a man wrapped in a gauzy shroud, whose mask is being cut away by a hand working a pair of scissors. Soon, however, in a move that presaged the interest in startling juxtapositions found in Longo's combines, he began to use dual monitors to pair up seemingly disconnected objects on his screens (for example, a water faucet and a screaming face in *The Artful Dodger* performance piece of 1976).

The role of video artist quickly lost its appeal for Longo. During a stint as video curator at New York's multimedia art center, The Kitchen, in 1978 and 1979, he was overwhelmed by the number of artists working in video and the feeling that "doing anything unorthodox was quickly becoming conventional." Muddy image quality and sound produced by the then-unsophisticated, low-tech equipment available was an additional frustration. Video, with its visible resolution, scan lines, and lighting trails, could not provide the visual satisfaction of the Rainer Werner Fassbinder and Jean-Luc Godard films Longo was consuming on a regular basis in lower Manhattan art-house cinemas. He also became fascinated by bands like James Chance and the Contortions, and the early Talking Heads and Television, who were emerging in downtown clubs in the late seventies and early eighties. Their experimentation was raw and visceral—nothing like the cool, heady detachment of an art world ruled by conceptualism. Longo himself played guitar during this period with the short-lived band Menthol Wars and other rock groups, thrashing out power chords alongside Glenn Branca, Richard Prince, and Rhys Chatham.

The one music and video exercise that was a portent of things to come was Longo's taping of a concert of No Wave bands organized by Michael Zwack at Artists Space in 1978. Each group was shot in the same, fixed angle from a camera mounted on the ceiling. While deadpan imagery was characteristic of the do-it-yourself, downtown Super 8 filmmaking of the period (notably in the films of Scott and Beth B, James Nares, Vivienne Dick, and Eric Mitchell), Longo's footage both subscribed to the dominant visual attitude and revealed how an interpretive sense of video could enhance the message of the music. Punky disenchantment warranted an equally noncommittal shooting style.

As Longo's attraction to video dwindled, drawing, painting, and performance became his main preoccupations. Performance in particular could combine film, slides, and video monitors with live action (or, in Longo's stasis-heavy pieces, inaction). Throughout his 1978 performance piece, *Sound Distance of a Good Man*, a still photograph composed after an image from Fassbinder's *The American Soldier* (page 17) was projected on film—a static shot in motion. For composer Rhys Chatham's Guitar Trio, in a performance at the Mudd Club in February 1979, Longo concocted an eighteen-minute slide show called *Pictures for Music*, a primitive exercise in making a music video. Joseph Hannan, a composer who has collaborated with Longo on many performance pieces, described the visuals as follows:

One picture will fade as another slowly comes into focus; we see six slides in all. A man flees down an alley; a woman hides her face on the shoulder of an anxious boy; a prop plane zooms past a silhouetted beacon and palm trees on a shore; an adult carries a dazed boy while horses are fed nearby. The images follow one another like the shots of a strictly ordered film. The possibility of narrative is distinct, for each of Longo's pictures has consequences to it; each suggests a before and after.[5]

The gradual progression of slides in *Pictures for Music*, and their open-ended, filmic effect, has a parallel in Longo's multipart painting-sculptures. The five-panel *Still* (1984; page 60) implies a filmic connection with its title alone. (Longo titles are often drawn from movies and songs, and pieces in different mediums sometimes share the same name: *Steel Angels* is both the title of Longo's two-part Metro Pictures show in 1986 and a proposed feature film, and there is *Arena Brains* the painting [fig. 6] as well as the featurette.) The serial grouping in *Still* links disparate images horizontally, arranging them for optimum impact rather than internal consistency: a hand clutching a bloody heart; a nude woman's back against a saturated red ground; a cropped bird of prey set to strike; a black granite-and-metal grid; a hammered relief of a soldier in armor on his horse.

Distinct from each other in size, color, and materials, this collection of "stills" is the painterly equivalent of radical film montage. If they were speeded up, they would form an image barrage, that agitated flux of visual information most aggressively present in Longo's New Order and Megadeth videos and *Arena Brains*. Each shot suggestively offers its own potential context or story, but instead of providing further details, it impatiently slaps against the next. The viewer is ordered to fill in the synapses or simply settle for disjunction.

As Longo has said of his Men in the Cities series, the large graphite-and-charcoal drawings of chic, black-clad lower Manhattanites striking contorted poses against blank backgrounds, "One of the reasons why the drawings became triptychs or groups of six or eight was not so much a relationship to Muybridge's sequential photographs, but much more like chord changes in a song. . . . It became a mission to find each pose that didn't necessarily make a sequence, but something much more elaborate, or abstract, like a fugue—like a rotation, or edits in a film, or news clips, or a commercial."[6]

Longo's tendency to pull other mediums into a discussion of any

Fig. 6. *Arena Brains,* 1985
Mixed media
96 x 36 in. (244 x 91.4 cm)
Collection Sue and Howard Simon,
New York

133

single one reveals not just his fluency in different disciplines—drawing, painting, sculpture, music, performance, film, photography—but the way they have interbred in his work over the years. He pushes all these forms to be informed by others as fully as possible, so that his art consistently spills over its boundaries: serial images become guitar chords become film stills become movies become songs, and back again. As Carter Ratcliff has observed, this interplay is supremely emblematic of Longo's work, which "re-enacts the conflicts that first bore his art into view—conflicts between people; incursions at the borders of mediums; high culture's struggle with low."[7]

Longo's refusal to accept the limitations of the singular image or form—as well as the conflict between the art world and popular culture—is present everywhere in his music videos. The predominant technique in the clips, next to quick editing, is layering. Dissolves and superimpositions abound. In the video for "Peace Sells" by Megadeth, a heavy-metal band that appeals mainly to teenage boys, Longo uses layered imagery to play on youthful ambivalence about war and power. A gleefully grating collage sets footage of the band, bobbing their long-locked heads on stage (and of fans hypnotically mimicking their movements), against a relentless montage of global war, protests, and violence. The elaborate meshing of imagery questions blind adherence to any dogma—whether political or simply the rabid attachment of a fan to a particular band. "Peace Sells" is an attack on subdued, pliable subjects—impressionable youth—launched within a medium that directly infiltrates their collective consciousness.

Likewise, in the video of "The One I Love" by R.E.M., superimposed pictures (of lovers' faces, a young man's mouth opening into a primal scream, images of trees, clouds, flowers) reinforce the video's central ideas: the clichéd idealism of romance and the anger that lurks beneath that Hallmark card-style depiction. Longo tempers his stylized, sentimental images (a beautiful young woman in a white slip, seated next to a floral arrangement, gazes wistfully into the distance) with intimations of amorous tension (the video bears a suggestive relation to Longo's violent lovers in the painting *Strong in Love* [1983; fig. 8]) and a climate out of control—interposed flashes of lightning, rapidly rolling cumulus clouds, orange sparks jumping along the image, threatening to break out into the "Fire" of the song's chorus. The images illuminate how "The One I Love" works at once as a conventional love song and as an embittered retort to that genre. Alternating male and female subjects, their heads occasionally overlapping, make even the identification of "the one" in "the one I love" unclear.

For Vernon Reid and Living Colour's "Middle Man" and World

Fig. 7. Still from "The One I Love,"
R.E.M., 1987

Fig. 8. *Strong in Love,* 1983
Acrylic and graphite on canvas
65 x 156 in. (165 x 395 cm)
Collection Bernd Klüser, Munich

Saxophone Quartet's "Hattie Wall," Longo's use of layering results in a jittery, interurban symphony. Living Colour is a rare example of a black band playing forceful rock-and-roll rather than rhythmic funk, while the Saxophone Quartet specializes in the complexity of the jazz saxophone. For "Middle Man," Longo followed up on the methods developed in "Peace Sells" by combining rapidly edited footage of the band in performance with a contextual picture of their origins— images of family, friends, ghetto neighborhoods, sixties' civil-rights activists. The camera's shock-zooms into murals on tenement walls

Fig. 9. Still from "Hattie Wall,"
World Saxophone Quartet, 1987

and depictions of poverty enforce the song's angry refrain "I'm just an ordinary middle man."

In the more elegant, restrained "Hattie Wall," Longo opens up the potentially static performance of four saxophone players by applying what he describes as a "stutter edit" to images of the instruments moving up and down, forcing a contrapuntal rhythm on the music. Dancer Bill T. Jones performs a jazzy solo turn, weaving in and out of circularly swerving footage of the players, emerging and disappearing in dissolves that smoothly fuse his movements to the melody. When the saxophones take a staccato turn, Longo switches from color footage to black-and-white, injecting his own lively mesh of signs, city, lights, and faces into the performance, each concluding musical phrase accompanied by a brief hold on an individual face.

Aside from these elaborate layerings, Longo toys with the small screen by splitting it in highly inventive ways, most notably in "Bizarre Love Triangle," where the screen divides vertically into four panels, each with a different moving picture struggling for attention against its neighbor and appearances by the British pop band New Order are either "shredded" (a random, time-base pattern, generated through a computer, makes images of the performers appear striated and "torn") or relegated to a small, horizontal strip at the bottom of the screen (fig. 10). This compressed space shows both the band in performance and an anonymous person's lips moving, interrupted by jolting edits and burdened by a much larger image of crowds above him. The relationship is similar to that of the sleek primer-gray building bearing down on the Pierrot figure in Longo's painting-relief *Pressure* (1982–83; pl. 29). (Longo likewise plays with the lip-synching convention in "The One I Love," where the head of singer Michael Stipe appears in profile, mouthing words that bear no relationship to the lyrics being sung.)

The public realm of the city, running on overactive movement, is a world of threat in "Triangle"—a worried-looking blond girl runs with her doll, a solitary tree quavers with apocalyptic resonance.

Figs. 10, 11. Still from "Bizarre Love Triangle," New Order, 1986

137

There is no room for the private, for romance. To carve a space for love, one has to slow things down, which is why the images in the song's chorus are surprisingly poignant: a couple like those in the Men in the Cities drawings floats down through a frame in a slow-motion free fall, twisting and tumbling in suspended grace against a bright blue sky. Their helpless resistance to gravity is a clear metaphor for the dehumanized speed of the epoch they live in. Arresting this temporal flux is daring, because it risks reflection.

For that reason, as well as to indulge a narrative tweak, Longo stems his high-velocity rush in "Triangle" by shutting off the music for a moment, mid-song, and inserting a brief black-and-white mock-*noir* love triangle of his own. A woman turns to a man to proclaim passionately: "I don't believe in reincarnation because I refuse to come back as a bug or a rabbit!" His dry reply: "Y'know, you're a real up person," is punctuated by the percolating return of the song, as the camera zooms into a second woman, who observes the exchange with a bored expression in the background. The coy vignette ripples the video's seamless surface, stalling the drive of the images.

Longo employs a similar device in "Peace Sells," where another black-and-white break serves to directly address impressionable teenage viewers. This time, the song halts to show a sullen teenage boy, sitting transfixed before a large television set that happens to be showing the Megadeth clip. His father enters the room, remote control in hand, and shouts: "What is this garbage you're watching? I want to watch the news!" The son retorts: "This IS the news," and turns the dial from a broadcast of Ronald Reagan back into the video.

If "Peace Sells" uses the music video to deploy a quick lesson on youth, war, and submission, Longo's subnarrative, *Arena Brains*, is an abbreviated treatise on the art world and the city. This thirty-four-minute film is an exorcism of sorts, where Longo dismantles the

Figs. 12,13. Stills from "Peace Sells," Megadeth, 1986

system he participates in, while both embracing and resisting a move toward narrative filmmaking. "You want to compete with the things that created you," says Longo. "I have this image of making a movie that would pop up in the middle of a *Dynasty*-style living room by Aaron Spelling, like the monster popping out of the man's stomach in *Alien*, saying: 'You made me, so here I am!' "

Arena Brains is precisely this mutant, the offspring of a television- and music-video-saturated head, well-versed in the films of Godard, Alfred Hitchcock, and David Lynch. Cowritten by Eric Bogosian, E. Max Frye, Emily Prager, Richard Price, and Longo, the film is the product of disparate sensibilities, each encouraged to tell a story in five minutes or less. The scenes are only tangentially related to one another, and shifts in locale are marked by the Longo signature— dramatic electric guitar chords. Here the artist makes material his analogy between serial imagery and progressive "chord changes in a song."

A visionary character called The Watcher (Michael Stipe) loosely binds the *Arena Brains* scenarios together. He dwells in a postindustrial barracks, full of drawings, maps, and clanging machinery, where he both receives and generates jangling image barrages that stem from his brain as though he's some bizarre human conductor. But the scenes he conjures up could not be more familiar: a smugly successful artist (Ray Liotta) and the critic who says he has made the artist's career (Richard Price) argue beneath New York's forbidding skyscrapers of commerce; an abusive stand-up comedian (Eric Bogosian) rants about success and greed (the scene is an obvious forerunner of Bogosian's work in the 1988 movie *Talk Radio*); a variety of image-conscious, distinctly eighties women trade platitudes in the ladies room of a nightclub; drugged-out rich kids try to steal a car radio; a loft party reveals quintessential one-upping dinner conversation; and a love affair is muted by a man's obsession with television. Finally these frustrations coalesce in a discharge of rage. And then The Watcher buys a sandwich in a late-night delicatessen, taking it home to eat in his bunker, where perhaps all this archetypal citified nastiness is no more than a bad, bad dream.

Arena Brains has a combative relationship to genre. With its filmic attention to camera movement, flat sit-com sets and dialogue, and music video-derived flashy cuts, *Arena Brains* draws on film, television, and video without adopting any of these forms entirely. What it does provide is a decided attack on the sterility of a power-hungry art world, with Longo turning at least some of the blame inward. The artist and dealer on the street are figures straight out of Men in the Cities, dressed in dark suits and even mimicking the drawings' images of struggle when the artist grabs his nemesis, kisses him, and spits

139

Figs. 14,15. Stills from
Arena Brains, 1987

out: "You're a good friend." In fact, Longo's drawings of tortured seventies downtowners bear a direct relationship to these more up-scale creatures of the eighties. In the past decade, the presence of suits and cocktail dresses in a downtown milieu have come to connote the fusion of art and commerce instead of low-cost, hip fashion—thrift-shop wear has been traded in for Issey Miyake and Giorgio Armani. These contemporary men in the cities stand for the posturing and hype of the marketplace.

This reflexive impulse reaches its apex in *Arena Brains* during the dinner-party scene, which was actually shot in Longo's studio with long-time assistant Diane Shea working on one of the artist's large drawings in the background. When the critic has a bizarre, seemingly epileptic seizure (or maybe it is just the result of a continually flashing Polaroid camera, manned by a brash self-promoter, played by Tom Gilroy), the artist immediately snatches the camera and takes a snap, places it in a projector, and begins to draw the enormous, grimacing face on the wall. While some might be tempted to read the scene as an egotistical act of self-aggrandizement on Longo's part, it is actually a pointed attack on blind self-interest, a symptom of callousness so extreme it is beyond irony.

Like much of Longo's work, *Arena Brains* is an inverted call to conscience. The vacant lives of control freaks and embittered urban-ites are not offered up as an exemplar of a glamorous life style, but as a case study in self-absorption and superficiality. These are prac-tically science-fiction creations, an undead created by the dislocating effects of media saturation. Thus *Arena Brains* can be viewed as a cautionary tale. This work and the music videos urge us to look critically at manipulative forms. Robert Longo's lab experiments in popular culture show that every product, no matter how canny, is vulnerable to attack from within.

VIDEOS AND FILMS

The music videos and film that follow were directed by the artist. The name of the performer or performing group precedes the title.

1986   Golden Palominos
          "Boy (Go)," Celluloid Records
          Produced by Melissa Lewis
          Edited by Gretchen Bender

          New Order
          "Bizarre Love Triangle," Factory Communications
          Produced by Michael Shamberg
          Edited by Gretchen Bender

          Megadeth
          "Peace Sells," Capitol Records
          Produced by Victoria Hamburg*
          Edited by Gretchen Bender

1987   *Arena Brains*, Elektra/Asylum Records
          34-minute film
          Premiered at the New York Film Festival, 1987
          Released on home video, 1988
          Produced by Victoria Hamburg and Jonathan Bender*
          Edited by Rick Feist
          Written by Eric Bogosian, E. Max Frye, Robert Longo, Emily Prager, and Richard Price

          R.E.M.
          "The One I Love," IRS Records

Produced by Victoria Hamburg*
Edited by Gretchen Bender
Nominated for Best Director, MTV Awards, 1988

"Wild Cards," MTV
Three art breaks, with dialogue
Produced by Victoria Hamburg*
Edited by Michael F. W. Collins

World Saxophone Quartet
"Hattie Wall," Elektra/Nonesuch Records
Produced by Victoria Hamburg*
Edited by Michael F. W. Collins

1988   Vernon Reid and Living Colour
          "Middle Man," Epic Records
          Produced by Victoria Hamburg*
          Edited by Michael F. W. Collins

          Rubén Blades
          "Hopes on Hold," Elektra Records
          Produced by Victoria Hamburg*
          Edited by Michael F. W. Collins

          Eric Bogosian
          "American Vanity," for *Vanity Fair* magazine
          10-minute video
          Produced by Victoria Hamburg*
          Edited by Gretchen Bender

*A Pressure Pictures, Ltd., production.

NOTES

1. This and all other unmarked quotations are from conversations between the author and Robert Longo, dating from spring 1986 to February 1989.
2. Gregory Lukow, "The Archaeology of the Music Video: Soundies, Snader Telescriptions, and Scopitones," catalogue of the 1986 National Video Festival, American Film Institute, Los Angeles, December 1986: 36.
3. Hal Foster, "Contemporary Art and Spectacle," in *Recodings: Art, Spectacle, Cultural Politics* (Port Townsend, Washington: Bay Press, 1985): 92.
4. Gregory Battcock, ed., *New Artists Video: A Critical Anthology* (New York: E. P. Dutton, 1978): xiv.
5. Joe Hannan, "Rhys Chatham's Guitar Trio with Robert Longo's Pictures for Music," *The Downtown Review* 1, no. 2 (April 1979): 22
6. "Save the Last Dance for Me," interview with Robert Longo by Richard Price, in *Men in the Cities, 1979–1982* (New York: Harry N. Abrams, 1986): 88–89, 91.
7. Carter Ratcliff, *Robert Longo* (New York: Rizzoli, 1985): 25. Ratcliff's essay also includes provocative meditations on the play between the still and the motion picture and on the idea of the monument in Longo's work.

Thanks to Paula Court for assistance in the preparation of this essay.

GOVERNING AUTHORITY: THE PERFORMANCE *EMPIRE*

BRIAN WALLIS

EDITOR'S NOTE: *When this essay appeared in the Summer 1982 issue of the art journal* Wedge, *it was among the first critical discussions of Robert Longo's performance works. Brian Wallis's essay focuses on* Empire, *a "performance trilogy" presented for the first time as a complete work in the atrium of The Corcoran Gallery of Art in Washington, D.C., on April 15, 1981. An astute analysis of the structure and form of* Empire, *the essay would seem to apply as easily to such recent performances as* Killing Angels, Solid Ashes, *and to the film* Arena Brains, *all of which continue to address themes of man's isolation within the social order, the seductiveness of power and authority, and the tyranny of cultural conformity.*

None of the protagonists comes to see that everything, thoughts, desires, dreams, arise directly from social reality or are manipulated by it.

R. W. Fassbinder

Power is always sustained more through communication than through force; less by the overt expression of specific ideologies or political opinions than through the deliberate use of sensorial seduction, circumventing intellectual reflection by the strategic replacement of discourse with sentiment. In his performance *Empire*, Robert Longo overturns conventional representation in order to expose the deliberate means by which aesthetic forms are converted into mechanisms

Fig. 1. Still from *Sound Distance of a Good Man,* 1978
In performance at the Franklin Furnace Archives, New York, 1978

143

of power. While on the surface *Empire* sustains interest as a grandly staged spectacle, a beautiful pageant play incorporating music, dance, film, and expressionistic lighting, Longo's ironic subtext is both a critique and a model of how these forms are used for social manipulation. As a critique the performance formulates, as an initial step in the governing of authoritarian power, a fundamental shift in aesthetic perception, away from symbolism or mimetic realism, toward the active criticism of the "activity of reference."

Longo develops his critical position by employing the representational forms he means to criticize, but he immediately makes clear that the reality of the performance is a simulated one. In the first tableau, *Sound Distance of a Good Man*, the performers (a pair of wrestlers and an opera singer) are presented not as characters but as imitations of what they represent. There is no attempt to inject meaning into their performances, no subjectivity on the part of Longo or the actors. Even the intense emotionality of the opera singer's aria is only a reenactment of a representation, so that no genuine passion is invested in it. Like all representations, the roles are imitations of imitations, structured and given meaning by their social context. Consequently, the forms of the representation are less an interpretation than a system of selection and critical presentation. In *Empire*, attention is drawn less to the image itself, the subject matter, than to the process and techniques by which it is formed.

Empire exaggerates reality while maintaining an illusion of order. The entire performance relies on extreme stylization. Meaning is dramatically heightened to the level of pure emotion, not through dialogue, but through alternate languages which exist outside narrative: heroic gesture, pose, lighting, music, and time. Abstract emotions are given spectacular form. The vignettes are not images of dramatic import, those which signal the climax or summarize a plot; they are purely rhetorical images which transmit only mood. But the operatic excess which characterizes the performance ultimately signals its underlying contradictions. For, although the music and staging suggest a monumental epic, no plot or narrative corroborates this effect.

Longo's images are like film stills, disjointed, isolated from context, loosened from their core of meaning. They provide fragmentary information and influence only through suggestion. Without the explanatory cloak of context, the performers' actions seem overdetermined and ambiguous. The apparent ambiguity of the images stems from their actual lack of meaning. The wrestlers in *Sound Distance of a Good Man* or the phalanx of waltzing couples in *Empire* are only vehicles for emotional manipulation, and as such, they dispense with the logical progression of language or narrative. By purging these images of their narrative context, Longo challenges the autonomy of narrative and the way it structures meaning through inference and false association. By isolating images and accentuating their artificiality, Longo begins the process of deconstruction.

The artificiality of the performance initiates, and in part depends upon, the audience's recognition of these images as reiterations of certain film types. Longo does not quote directly from film, but re-invents images in a way that makes them *seem* familiar by reproducing the style and rhythm of film. Film is an appropriate analogue for Longo's deconstructive strategy, for it is largely through film that

Fig. 2. *Surrender*, 1979
In performance at The Kitchen, New York, 1979

the autonomy of social stereotypes is erected. Film is the mythic structure of the twentieth century; it is the public medium, and thus it has provided the perfect forum for the gentle shaping of ideological and social attitudes. Further, film's basis in photography lends a special credibility to the images which, even if constructed, appear real. The surfeit of factual information in film, both in quantity and heightened quality, prompts an easy acceptance of its fiction over an impoverished reality. This allows film, particularly the more popular genres such as melodrama and science fiction, to be overlaid with strata of connotations posing as "generally accepted" values. In its appeal to mass audiences film frequently reverses the actual order of things (the extraordinary is made ordinary: as in death made banal through repetition) and promotes certain attitudes (domesticity, patriarchal order, democracy), while deviants from this norm are marginalized. Film then is not a passive presentation but involves enticement, manipulation, and complicity.

Longo's own films, projected in the center of the first two tableaux, might be seen as the logical terminus of his essentially filmic style, in which stasis is equated with critical observation. For each of these films consists of only a single image: a fifteen-minute fixed-frame shot of a still photograph. The films articulate not only their specific fixed images (images of nostalgia and loss: a businessman apparently being shot, a ruined Greek statue), but also Longo's deconstruction of the scaffold of technical properties which film generally employs: motion, editing, depth of field, montage, sound-image synchronization. By eliminating these qualities from his film, Longo calls into question their purpose and function. In their stark, documentary style the single-image films contrast with the lush visual style of the performance. They are extremes of filmic potential: on the one hand, the austere, totally reduced core image, on the other hand, the superficial gloss, the extra-narrative effects skimmed from the illusion.

Such contrasts characterize the complexity of *Empire*. Longo is aware of the irony of things not being what they seem, and *Empire* is composed of ambiguities and contradictions: films which project static images, wrestlers who seem to be embracing, paired dancers who seem ignorant of their partners. These specific ambiguities are signs of the more general and unsettling contradiction of the performance, the contrast between the lure of the imagery through the dramatic uses of music, gesture, and lighting and the distancing effects of the narrator, the lack of narrative continuity, and the imposition of static films. The confrontation of these cross purposes creates the principle tension that animates the performance and raises an unsettling skepticism. The mediation of representational forms in society tends to resolve all ambiguities, to reduce contradictions to patterns, and in this way to integrate man into society and to reassure him. By reinserting and heightening these differences; Longo lifts the mask that conceals meaning and motivation in the use of representation.

Although I have suggested that there is no real meaning or subject matter to be inferred from Longo's performance tableaux, this is not exactly true. It is evident that through the poetic associations of the vignettes and the oblique cues of the narrator each of the tableaux stands as a metaphor for the way in which manipulation occurs.

Fig. 3. *Empire: Sound Distance of a Good Man,* 1978
In performance at The Corcoran
Gallery of Art, Washington, D.C.,
1981

There is a progression from the initial scenes of beauty and overwhelming emotional appeal to the final sequence of mass participation, from isolation to assimilation and from personal expression
and communication to conformity. As a group the three tableaux
represent the pattern of manipulation: seduction, yielding, and conformity. This can also be seen as a temporal sequence, in which the
tableaux represent the choices of the past (*Sound Distance of a Good
Man*: precedents, memory, nostalgia), present (*Surrender:* decision-
making, requiring judgment, order, action), and future (*Empire*: consequences, hope, contemplation). But these meanings remain elu-
sive, seeming perhaps too weighty for the evanescent and baroque
images of *Empire*. Its symbols remain fluid, dreamlike and enigmatic,
beckoning the viewer but denying satisfaction.

The structure of the performance mirrors the subject matter, the
two existing simultaneously, one the overt image of manipulation,
the other physically manipulating the audience and its perception
and participation. Like the propagandistic spectacles which *Empire*
in part emulates, Longo's performance depends to a large extent on
the psychic impact of formal structure to effect the seduction of the
audience. The logic of the symmetrical trilogy, especially conforming
to the tripartite atrium of The Corcoran Gallery of Art in Washington,
D.C., provides a pattern denied by the missing narrative. The rigid
structuring of the performance acts as a restraint to the intense emotionality promoted by the music and gesture, and it is calming in its
reassurance of resolution. The staging of the tableaux in separate
areas of the atrium also requires the audience to participate in the

147

structure, actually moving from location to location and in this way physically yielding to the involvement in the illusions of the performance.

By scattering his meaning, by making the images deliberately ambiguous and by focusing more on the authoritarian structure of the spectacle than on its climaxes, Longo forces responsibility for the performance on the audience. The converging vectors of meaning do not focus on the artist, but on the audience. Acceptance of the general circumstances of the performance involves the complicity of the audience. Out of resignation and habit, the audience accepts one false image after another, convinced by the heroic scale and encouraged by the need to establish a logical order. In this way, the audience is involved as a participant in the performance, the victim of manipulation metaphorically spelled out in the imagery. Longo turns the responsibility onto the individual members of the audience, making the real meaning their willingness to question not only the received values of a governing authority but also their own too-ready willingness to accept these values.

Longo's performance is situated in the juncture where the dependence on the personal, experimental, and psychological is giving way to a more explicitly political and historically necessitated method. In realizing that traditional means of artmaking are insufficient and outmoded, Longo attempts to revitalize and reorient the activity of representation. The meaning of art can no longer be fixed, a personal sign with a stamp of finality. Rather it must be a process, a process of social awareness and criticism, not self-consciousness. Its process lies in the creation of a field of understanding, a matrix of presentation and demonstration rather than expression and display. Power and its abuse remain the most pressing subjects for contemporary artists, making clear their necessity to open a space, allowing for the exposure of society's shameless contradictions and the devices used to mask them. This requires the subversion and reuse of traditional forms, a decentering to reveal the structure of representational systems. By appropriating forms and quoting images, Longo gives meaning to the simple act of recognition and criticism. The individual artist yields in significance to a collaborative social activity. Longo's ambivalence toward his performance, then, is encouraging; his position cleaves the boundary between the amorality of the media and the overwrought position of the expressionist artist.

APPENDIX:THREE PERFORMANCES

EMPIRE
A Performance Trilogy

Premiered April 15, 1981, in the atrium of The Corcoran Gallery of Art,
Washington, D.C.
Written and directed by Robert Longo
Music by Brian Eno, Peter Gordon, Joseph Hannan
Performers: Speaker—Eric Bogosian;
Wrestlers—Eric Barsness, Bill T. Jones; Opera Singer—Peggy Atkinson;
Saxophone Player—Peter Gordon; Jet Boy and Jet Girl—Joseph Hannan,
Adela Basayne-Smith; Man in Film—Bernard Tschumi
Running time: approximately 65 minutes

The audience enters to slowed, ecstatic music. The house lights fade out and
a spotlight focuses on the Speaker, upstage center.

Speaker: Good evening, ladies and gentlemen. Welcome to The Corcoran
Gallery of Art, which this evening is presenting the premier of *Empire: A Performance Trilogy* by Robert Longo.

The Speaker begins to walk forward; we hear the sound of his heels on the
floor as he walks to downstage center; he is a solicitous host.

Speaker: My name is Eric Bogosian. It is my pleasure this evening to be your
host. *Empire* is divided into three parts: *Sound Distance of a Good
Man, Surrender,* and *Empire.* These individual components have
been created over the past three years. Tonight, for the first time,
they will be performed together, to become one. The three sections of *Empire* take place in various locations in the atrium; each
section is meant to be viewed from a specific distance and location. In my introductions, I will guide you to the best vantage
points. Please feel free to explore the various angles from which
the action may be viewed.

The Speaker turns and walks back the way he came. Upstage, he turns back,
becoming a character.

Speaker: La statua si erigerà come le statue si erigeranno. A statue will stand like statues stand, and every day will be like every other. And now we begin with *Sound Distance of a Good Man.*

I. Sound Distance of a Good Man
(Premiered April 18, 1978, at Franklin Furnace Archives, New York)

A three-sectioned, twenty-four-foot platform with light-gray sides and a black top is set between two columns. A movie screen is positioned above the center section. The action of the three parts fades in, forming a sculptural-cinematic triptych.

To the left, on a level above the other two sections, an amber spotlight fades in on two men in a tight embrace, a frozen pose; after a few seconds they start to move, choreographed in a very slow act of wrestling. They are positioned on a revolving disk, sixty inches in diameter, which makes a complete turn every thirty seconds. The two wrestlers are matched in size, but contrast visually—blond hair and fair skin/brown hair and dark skin. Their appearance refers to past cinema—the wrestling scene in Ken Russell's *Women in Love,* Bruce Lee's shirtless karate costume and shining skin. The two go through a series of traditional wrestling moves, their actions charged with eroticism, turning under the light like ballerinas in a music box.

A nine-by-twelve-foot image is projected in black-and-white sixteen millimeter film onto the screen in the center. Showing no motion except for the grain and flickering of the film, the upper torso of a man, body arching in convulsion, is set in contrast to the immobile statue of a lion and the motionlessness of the picture itself.

To the right, and on a level below the other two sections, an overhead spotlight fades in (deep purple) on an elegant woman in a long, white, off-the-shoulder dress. She, too, is frozen in a pose, statuesque. As the wrestlers' platform begins to revolve, she starts to sing in an operatic *forte,* supported by the music (Brian Eno's slowed-down version of Pachelbel's Canon) and other prerecorded voices. She is the siren, the power source beckoning the audience; the voices combine with the music to fill the room with a thick atmosphere of theater and cinema.

The tableau takes its course; after fifteen minutes, the wrestlers freeze, their revolving platform stops, the woman stops singing, the spots fade, and the film fades as the total set returns to sculpture.

Darkness. Pause. The Speaker is now standing on the landing of the grand staircase leading to the upper atrium. The audience rises to move up the stairs. They are restrained by ushers at the foot of the staircase while the Speaker continues:

Speaker: Mesdames et messieurs. Attention, s'il vous plaît.

The Speaker makes a transition to a character—he is slowly becoming more and more Rod Serling-like, introducing us to a twilight zone. He tells a story.

Speaker: A streetlight, the night in the city, the lone sound of a saxophone spills out from the door of a cafe, time stands still, a man, a woman, a story.

The Speaker turns and walks upstairs. At the top landing, he turns and says:

Speaker: You are now invited to climb these stairs for the presentation of *Surrender*.

The spotlight cuts, and he exits. Lights come up on the steps, one by one. The ushers now allow the audience to ascend to the viewing area.

Empire: Surrender, 1979
In performance at The Corcoran
Gallery of Art, Washington, D.C.,
1981

II. Surrender
(Premiered May 1979 at The Kitchen, New York)

Two glossy black runways are each illuminated from above by three spotlights. Centered at the far end of the runways is a black wall unit. On the upper half of the wall is a ten-by-fourteen-foot film screen.

The house lights dim to total blackness. Pause. The sound of a saxophone blasts out in the dark. A spotlight comes on, silhouetting a saxophone player in a black mohair suit, who leans in a doorway as he plays. He pivots mechanically, straddling the doorsill. Powerful light floods him from behind, projecting his shadow. He is now playing a clear R & B Junior Walker-style riff. He walks into the room and, robotlike, approaches the runway at the right. As he takes his first step onto the runway, there is simultaneous action on the film screen and the other runway. The six overhead spots fade in, creating three pools of light on each runway.

On the runway at the left the spots reveal a man and woman nattily dressed in black, frozen in a pose, matching the placement of the saxophone player opposite them. A film of a Greek statue—a victorious young athlete, his arms now broken off—fades in on the screen as the saxophone player enters the first spotlight on his runway. In slow motion, the man and woman begin to dance.

The saxophone player moves down his runway at the same time as the dancers. Gradually, as he passes through the spots, his music and gestures change. The mechanical R & B becomes more lucid, his saxophone more

151

Still from *Empire: Surrender,* 1979
In performance at The Corcoran
Gallery of Art, Washington, D.C.,
1981

soothing, as he approaches and moves through the second spot. His movements become more abstract, and his music screeches as he nears the third spot.

The man and woman begin a slow-motion popular dance from the fifties. They turn in each other's arms. As they move through their spotlights, their dance evolves into a conflation of dance history: fifties, sixties, and disco.

The motionless film image of the oversize statue acts as a colossal guardian.

The man and woman freeze under the last spotlight; the saxophone player is still as his music calms down to a simple melody. The spotlights and film fade. The saxophone melody continues in darkness and then fades.

After the performance, there is brief pause before the lights come up on the Speaker, now in the north end of the lower atrium. He can be seen from the performance space upstairs. He appears to be in reverie and does not look up at the audience.

Speaker: In the past I often had anxiety dreams in which I plunged hundreds of meters down unending facades of buildings. Here, I am spared that sort of thing.

Silence. Out of the silence, a sound becomes a laugh. The Speaker laughs quietly, then demoniacally, as he turns his eyes up to look at the spectators. He is now an emcee character.

Speaker: Meine Damen und Herren, sind glücklich. Die Ende is nahe. Kommen Sie, bitte. Culture is not a burden, it is an opportunity. It begins with order, grows with liberty, and dies in chaos. And now our final picture, *Empire,* may be viewed from your present situation or from here—below—in these seats.

The spotlight on the Speaker fades as the audience returns to the lower atrium.

152

Empire, 1981
In performance at The Corcoran
Gallery of Art, Washington, D.C.,
1981

III. Empire

(Premiered April 15, 1981, at The Corcoran Gallery of Art, Washington, D.C.)

A rank of lights—fifteen to twenty small pinpoint spots—are equally spaced on a twenty-five-foot horizontal shaft. During the course of the performance, the shaft ascends from floor level to eight feet; the shaft also rotates ninety degrees so that the beams of light, originally directed toward the ceiling, turn to shine out over the observers' heads. Four large loudspeakers, such as might be used in a movie theater, are positioned invisibly in the corners.

The audience is seated at the far end of the gallery. The ranks of light slowly fade in, synchronized with the entrance of fanfarelike music for brass, strings, and organ. The ranks form pillars of light like those made by searchlights against the night sky. As the lights approach their brightest level, the music peaks and sustains chords. The ranks of light ascend as the music shifts to a bright, martial processional. At eight feet, the ranks slowly rotate so that the rays beam out over the heads of the observers, creating a ceiling of light.

From the dark areas under the lights, dancing couples emerge in evening dress; they are first seen filing in from the right, man-woman-man-woman. The music has assumed the rhythm and phrasing of a waltz. The couples begin their regimented steps, waltzing slowly and mechanically toward the audience. Lines of couples enter at closer and closer intervals; the music accelerates as the dancers approach in waves. The first group slows as it reaches the audience, uncomfortably close; the later groups follow, creating a wall of swaying, silhouetted bodies. An air-raid siren pierces the music. As it builds, the music abruptly halts, breaking the atmosphere; the lights cut off. In the darkness, the siren continues to wail and then segues to another sound—the clarion call of trumpets transforming the ballroom into a battlefield. The dancers scurry to marked exits. The houselights rise and the music fades. The audience exits to a view of the Ellipse and the White House.

Edited by Howard Halle and Brian Wallis

KILLING ANGELS
A Performance in Two Parts

Premiered October 16, 1987, at Burchfield Art Center,
State University College, Buffalo, New York
Conceived and directed by Robert Longo
Music by Stuart Argabright, Joseph Hannan, Robert Longo
Choreography by Bill T. Jones, Arnie Zane, Adrienne Altenhaus
Video artists: Gretchen Bender, Michel Auder, Douglas Sloan,
Robert Longo
Scenic design by Stephen Brownless
Multiimage projections by Douglas Sloan, ICON Communications, Ltd.
Texts for *Marble Fog* by Eric Bogosian and Robert Longo; texts for *Lead Sun*
by Tom Gilroy, Robert Longo, Richard Schiff, and Joseph Hannan
Performers: Three Sentinels—Adrienne Altenhaus, Damian Aquavella,
Sean Curran
Pacer—Eric Bogosian (prerecorded); God Face—Vito Acconci;
New Past—Vito Acconci; Woman in Black Dress—Megan Emory; Sax Captain—Steve Elson; Solo Dancer—Bill T. Jones; Actors—Tom Gilroy, Richard Schiff; Opera Singer—Peggy Atkinson; Young Girl—Monica Murphy
Running time: approximately 90 minutes

I. Marble Fog

(Premiered April 13, 1985, at The Brooklyn Museum)
The audience enters to the sound of slow, three-chord piano music. The
stage is bare except for a huge screen divided into four sections—a horizontal panel covers the top third and three vertical panels divide the lower part.

1. Landscape, Flowers, and Blue Skies
Panoramic projections of American scenes—mountains and fields of flowers—dissolve slowly into blue skies across the top screen. The music is majestic, Aaron Copland-esque.

2. Buildings
The blue sky fills the entire top screen and then bleeds down to fill all four
panels. The music tumbles into a dirgelike hymn of quaking sound. The
three bottom screens dissolve into projections of monolithic skyscrapers—cathedrals of the new world—and the top of building after building is
silhouetted against blue skies; the top screen remains blue.

3. Three Sentinels
The buildings cross-fade into three giant silhouettes of live performers. The
blue skies become an oscilloscope reading of a heartbeat. The left and right
figures, both men, move their arms in synchronized semaphoric gestures.
The woman in the center makes gestures reminiscent of ritualistic statues. As
she speaks, she assumes the voices of stereotypical characters—an airline
stewardess, a rock star, or an evangelist.

Woman: Totally sky
      Totally sky
      The landscape was totally sky
      Empty bodies empty houses empty heads
      A land of motors and motion
      Everything I see is blown through with smoke
      Everything is on fire everywhere
      Ten thousand years of solid collision
      A bare wasteland of raw savage rock
      And everything was on fire
      It doesn't matter that memory distorts
      Every image every sound comes back out of the smoke
      With the smell of things burning
      Total it up in the crowded sky
      We want God. We want mass comfort. We want touch
      I'm totally yours
      Under the total sky
      We have time and time is money
      And this is the kind of money we all should have
      Brighter color, faster cars, whiter whites, and all major credit cards
      Talking about talk

Killing Angels: Marble Fog, 1987
In performance at Burchfield Art
Center, State University College,
Buffalo, New York, 1987

155

Everything I've ever known was from books
These are the tender gestures of life
These are the words you hear when words are too much
This is where dream and rumor speak
Love respects fear
Touch my heart
Talking about talking about talk
Know the rules. Learn the lines
Same as it ever was. Same as it ever was
Rock the house
Shake the land
Talk that talk
Be all that you can be
We are the world
Jumping from the eyes of God
We are the world
Jumping from the eyes of God
("Crowded God" by Robert Longo)

The screen over the triptych of live performers turns to a projection of words. The texts, in different languages, are cleanly printed, just as the woman's voice and the guitar and drum that accompany her are clean and unhurried. As her reading gets more and more intense, the music grows fuller and louder. Cued by sound effects of breaking bottles, flying planes, and falling bombs, the words on the screen become marked, mutilated, and fragmented, and eventually turn into a huge computer-graphic landscape. Everything becomes chaotic, disjointed. The woman rants. The guitars and drums are pounding. The two men, like military archetypes, remain strong, machinelike.

Killing Angels: Marble Fog, 1987
In performance at Burchfield Art
Center, State University College,
Buffalo, New York, 1987

4. Red T

The center and top screens turn red and form an enormous red "T." The woman's head remains visible. On either side, where the male performers stand, great abstract scribbles are projected around them. Eventually the whole stage fades into darkness. Only the heads of the three performers remain lit. The scrim turns red, and the shadow of the silent woman dances like Salome to piano music.

5. Green Scene

The stage lights fade from red to green. Across the top screen, news photos are projected, bathed in green—a plane crash, an operating room, a riot. Behind the scrims, a crowd of people is gathered. They stare zombylike at the audience.

Out of the stillness, the voice of the Pacer begins to rant like a street preacher.

Pacer: Yeah, yeah, yeah, yeah, yeah, yeah, yeah. Sure, sure, sure, sure, sure, sure. They're always tellin' you the same old story. They're always givin' you the same old story. One plus one equals two, two plus two equals four. You reap what you sow, it always starts the same way, it always ends the same way. Ya goin', ya comin', ya goin', ya take it, ya leave it, ya make it, ya need it, it's human nature. It's human nature. It's always the same ol' story. Same ol' story. Man against man, man against nature, man against himself. Beginning, middle, end. Climax, anticlimax, subplot . . .

It's dog eat dog, man eat man, eat meat, hunt the meat, meets the letter of the law, the law of the land, and the land is a jungle. Look, I gotta look after me first. I gotta worry about me. They say give to the taxes, give to the starving children, give to the abandoned babies, the blind people, the poor people. I see 'em on TV.

It's just getting harder and harder and harder. Every day, day in and day out ya gotta stand in line, ya gotta stand in line for hours and hours. And then ya get to the end of the line, ya get to the end of the line, they say, they say, they say, no more, no more, we don't got no more for you. No more for you. For who? Who . . . wh . . who's gettin' it, who's gettin' it? I'm not. I not gettin' it. You either winnin' or you losin', ya sinkin' or ya swimmin', an' I'm sinkin' see? I . . I . . I'm in a little lifeboat and I'm in the middle of the ocean and I'm sinkin'. I'm a little piece a ice that's gettin' smaller and smaller and smaller every day, day in, day out. I'm floatin' in that water. . . .

Sink or swim, fish or cut bait. You're either part a the problem or ya part a the solution. And what's a solution, huh? What's a solution, the bomb? The bomb? Drop the bomb, that's what I say. Drop the bomb. I'm not waitin' for no packages. I got no all expense-paid vacation, I'm no little Orphan Annie, 'tomorrow, tomorrow, tomorrow . . .'

Where's the tomorrow, huh, you got a tomorrow? I don't got no tomorrow. More, more, more, more, more that's tomorrow, that's what tomorrow is, more right? More, more, we gotta make some more money. Let's make some more money, then we can buy some more houses. We gotta buy a lot more houses, then we can have some more kids. And then we gotta have some more TV sets for the kids so then we can have some more TV stations. That's what we need, a lot more TV stations. UHF, VHF, cable TV, satellite, mini, maxi, tape deck, TBS, CBS, cable TV, everywhere you go the music's playin', the TV's playin', it's too loud, it's too loud, shut it off. I can', I can'. Stop . . SHUT UP! Shut up, just shut up! [background noise fades in]

("Pacer," from *Funhouse,* written and performed by Eric Bogosian)

Fade to black as the sound of a door shutting cuts off the Pacer's shouting voice.

6. God Face

A distorted face is projected in a "T"-shape onto the top and central panels of the screen. The eyes and mouth are made up like a geisha or a Pierrot. The eyes and mouth move as the face speaks. The voice is distorted, mechanical and deeply resonant. On the left and right sides of the mouth are two panels of star fields. From this deep space, figures seem to jump out of the God Face, momentarily caught by strobe lights. The God Face speaks, reading:

God Face: You are an old man who thinks in terms of nations and peoples. There are no nations! There are no peoples! There are no Russians. There are no Arabs! There are no third worlds! There is no West! There is only one holistic system of systems, one vast and immense interwoven, interacting, multivariate, multinational dominion of dollars! Petro-dollars, electro-dollars, multidollars! Reich marks, rubles, pounds, and shekels!
It is the international system of currency that determines the totality of life on this planet! That is the natural order of things today! That is the atomic and subatomic and galactic structure of things today! And you have meddled with the primal forces of nature, and you will atone!

(Excerpt from *Network,* by Paddy Chayefsky)

The voice collapses like a machine when the plug has been pulled and the power dies. It is replaced by the sound of someone breathing in an oxygen tent or in outer space. The God Face dissolves into blackness. For the first time, the scrim in the center opens and reveals the darkness and depth of the stage.

7. Geisha

From out of the darkness, taking the traditional tiny steps, the geisha appears. The light forms an egg-shaped oval around her. The breathing sound reverberates in a harmonic rhythm around the auditorium. The geisha, in

Killing Angels: Marble Fog, 1987
In performance at Burchfield Art
Center, State University College,
Buffalo, New York, 1987

whiteface, stands motionless for over a minute. She is still and silent as her eyes deliberately scan the audience from behind her white makeup.

The lights dim, and the sound fades. The geisha returns to the darkness at center stage.

II. Lead Sun

Entr'acte. Video: "A Life in a Day"

Video walls come out from either side of the stage and join together at center stage to form a bank of sixty-four monitors. The music is reminiscent of a Roman circus—all procession and pageantry. An image barrage, compiled from news broadcasts on network, local, and cable TV during one day, is played simultaneously on all the monitors. The light from the video wall fills the theater. When the video ends, the wall of monitors splits and slides offstage.

1. Planet Roll

In the darkness, there is the sound of white noise. In a horizontal wedge of golden light, filled with smoke—like a crack in the universe—a woman floats like an astronaut free of gravity. She is wearing a black strapless dress. The white noise deepens to a rumble. At left, thirty feet above the stage, she moves slowly, as if awakening, while a large, golden planet rolls out from the same side of the stage. The rumbling comes from the glowing sphere. It is being pushed by seven muscular nude men and women.

The light hits the edge of a huge ball like the reflection of sunrise on a planet. The seven people strain to roll and contain the orb's weight on its course across the stage.

Simultaneously, at the back of the audience, an elegantly dressed man with a red electric guitar modulates the loud rumble of the planet into a heavy-metal serenade. Like a conjurer, he seems to pull the ball across the stage with his music. The music is physical and gestural, punctuated by

159

screeching and wailing guitar effects. He walks down the right aisle and is hit by a vertical beam of light as he steps onto the stage. The planet has rolled off-stage. He plays a beautiful, melodic song to the woman, who has come to life and responds to the music by spinning faster and faster like a needle hanging from a thread. The guitar player drops to his knees in front of her to complete the serenade. The velocity of the scene increases until it vanishes into blackness.

2. Heavenly   Poobah

An army of twenty-five saxophone players is set in blackness against a starry night.

The musicians are on their knees, backs to the audience. As they raise their instruments in unison, light hits the saxes to form halos over their heads. They rise, playing a dirge, and turn around, again in unison. The players, all uniform in size and height, wear black suits and ties, white shirts, and hold tenor saxophones—black, white, and gold. In a surreal phalanx, they move ominously forward. The captain in the center of the line comes toward the audience, pulling the line of musicians into a V-shape.

The music turns into a doo-wop chorus, and the captain leads the lines through a choreographed dance. It is in the tradition of the marching band, one musician multiplied into many, à la Busby Berkeley. At the end of the number, the musicians form a row across the stage; light streams across the saxophones. They split and exit until only the captain remains. He walks to the back of the stage, saxophone wailing, until he fades into darkness.

Entr'acte. Video: "Island: Angels Made for RL"

A bird flying, a fish, just caught, flops in its own blood. Mounted police at night at an intersection—the street is wet and shining. A shark swims by, as though the monitors were an aquarium. Reshot television footage flashes by. A sunset; a young girl wipes a window clear, which turns into car windshield wipers; an open road in a bleak winter landscape. Everything about it is different from what we have seen and will see. We are at the center of the performance's duration.

3. Red Room

A huge, red silk curtain is knotted in the center. It is reminiscent of the backdrop for a political rally. It begins to move, gradually creating a breathing, throbbing womb. The sound of a monstrous machine grinding and churning awakens a solitary man, who is lying face-down in the middle of the stage. As the sound becomes more melodic and then turns into an orchestral statement, the dancer rises like a machine or a robot and becomes fluid, spreading his arms like a swan or eagle in flight.

The red curtain creates an evocative partner for the dancer. His movement—powerful and naturalistic, but on a human scale—responds to the giantism of the set and the previous scenes. The dancer is the sole performer; his performance is a tribute to man and the human body as an ultimate machine.

The dance ends as it began; and the dancer sinks back into the floor.

Killing Angels: Lead Sun, 1987
In performance at Burchfield Art
Center, State University College,
Buffalo, New York, 1987

4. Detritus Gomi / Hall of Confusion

An actor, posing as a stagehand, comes onstage and claims to have been fired. Another actor, the stage manager, tries to drag him off so the performance can continue. While they argue, props and garbage are thrown onstage and chaos ensues. An opera singer rises from the orchestra pit singing "Ah, fors'è lui" from *La Traviata.* The video wall comes part way out, and as the curtain closes, the argument between the two actors is broadcast on the video wall.

Eventually, the stage manager tells the opera singer to "shut up." She returns to the pit; the lights fade to black.

5. Matrix Mutants

The curtain opens to the sound of wind, thunder, and a deep, rumbling chorus of voices. A huge orange Day-Glo grid stands against a dark-blue backdrop. A single dead tree is at left—all that remains in the postnuclear wasteland. Three silhouettes of mutants emerge. One has three heads, the body of the second is a round ball, and the third has a grotesquely elongated neck. They reinterpret the gestures of the three sentinels in *Marble Fog.* This time the movements are no longer symmetrical but skewed and are abstracted against a background of desolation. The deep, resonant voice of a man envelops the scene:

Voice of the new past: I remember the days of blue skies and green grass,
Yellow sun.
Now the sky is the color of television
tuned to a dead channel.
I walk through the wreckage of the future
and I change the past.
Now I'm alone.
I long for the touch of flesh.
The flesh that strategic disease has destroyed.

I remember the days of 24-hour cycles,
of power and money,
of rich and poor,
of good and bad.
Where is the traditional value we built a nation on?
I was always afraid of the end
So I prolonged a dead middle just to save a
tomorrow.
My aim was disguised as love,
And love all things I did
In that special way
Like a boy
and a new toy.
But toys break,
And break I did
Over and over and over
Like a machine in love.
Never does the pain go away.
In the silver tides of phosphenes
I travel the tracks of bloodlines.
The matrix has replaced my life.
I live in a representation of an original
That has no origin.
A copy of a copy of a copy of a copy of a copy.
And history died when the copy became content.
In dead time
In dead cities
Dead eyes
Tell stories of days that never were.
The world was a business.
In civil war
Confusion became my God.
I measured time with blood.
I lived in the forest of world banks.
I walked with panthers.
Life was glamorous.
Drugs and blue skies
Super religion
Arena of atomic lies
Built on guilt.
I am moving so fast
I'm standing still
From the base of my scull
My brain has a gray glow.
The ragged cascade of images that
Never once
Made any sense to me.
I had visions.

A message was being sent
A life as a receiver
I've always had a longing for the real thing,
And real was too much for me.
Take me
Hold me
Make my body rest
In the sleep of dead lights
Of forever
An object of no use
Tune in Turn off Burn out
Forever
An object of no use
Forever
An object of no use
Forever.

During the speech, a continuous procession of fourteen-foot mutants with long legs and pointed heads crosses the stage, against the Day-Glo grid. Their gait, robotic and grand, is in rhythm with the voice. The voice

Killing Angels: Lead Sun, 1987
In performance at Burchfield Art
Center, State University College,
Buffalo, New York, 1987

dies, like a machine that has been shut off, and the scene fades into darkness.

Entr'acte. Video: "Inside the Machine"
Computer-generated images of geometric and abstract landscapes perform a ballet of mathematically inspired shapes and artificial colors. The images are completely synthesized—made without a camera. The music is as electronic as the images. A world of completely artificial appearances—a cartoon of calculations—a landscape that does not exist in the physical world.
6. Abstract's Future
Visible at right in the orchestra pit is a violist, and at left, a flutist; a pianist is unseen. They play a three-chord sequence as the curtain opens.

The background is dusky blue. A rusted, eighteen-foot cube is suspended from one of its corners. A young girl in a party dress stands at stage right. She sings, accompanied by the instruments. Her voice sets the cube slowly rotating. Her song turns into a list of spoken statements, ending with "Who lives on earth now?" The lights fade to a single spot on her face and then to black.

The scrims slide onstage, and the credits are projected.

Edited by Victoria Hamburg, Jennifer Cox, and Joseph Hannan

SOLID ASHES
A Collaborative Theater Work

Premiered October 17, 1988, at the Rotterdamse Schouwburg, Rotterdam
Written and directed by Robert Longo, Paul Gallis, and Janine Brogt
Music by Stuart Argabright, Philip Glass, Joseph Hannan, Colin McPhee,
and Arvo Pärt
and performed by the Rotterdam Philharmonic Orchestra,
conducted by Reinbert de Leeuw
Running time: approximately 120 minutes

Solid Ashes is a modern version of the Hercules myth, set in the near future. Hercules's world is controlled by the Nuclear Nine Corporation, a political-economic power block. The action takes place in a part of the world that is still fit for human life. The script is written in many languages, as though all languages had become one and were comprehensible to all.

I. Family Album: A Weekend

Curtain opens to reveal a giant, fresh green hedge that occupies all but the top fourth of the proscenium, which is sky blue. From behind the hedge, chain saws can be heard. First the top six inches of the hedge are cut, falling to the floor. The scent permeates the theater. The chain saw then appears to be cutting the hedge in a "V" shape down the center. The open "V" space reveals H. [Hercules] dressed in a work suit and goggles, with the stage behind.

The "V" parts stage right and left. Sections of houses in the style of Gordon Matta-Clarke are revealed in a forced perspective, which divides the stage diagonally and enables the audience to see both inside and out. Men and women perform tasks that are associated with masculine and feminine activities: men at the left, outside and on the lawn; women to the right, inside. Beautiful clouds travel through the blue sky.

H. climbs out of his work suit and is dressed conservatively in a business suit and tie. He says: "Honey, I'm home." Outside, men play sports, fix cars, and drink beer. H. plays with his children. His wife M. [Megara] and the other women inside are going about their daily chores. The atmosphere on stage is like that of a carnival. Among the thirty people on stage, six sets of twins appear and reappear throughout the performance.

M. begins to speak. Her text is comprised mainly of fragments from newspapers, magazines, and memories. The outside world is presented as hostile, chaotic, and violent. Her private world is centered on her extraordinary husband, about whom she tells us.

The house fragments shift from stage right to left to reveal an enormous kitchen interior. The chorus of men and women begins to disappear; H. and M. prepare to enjoy each other's company when the "Board" appears. The boardroom table forces its way into the scene from stage right, complete

Solid Ashes, 1988
In performance at Rotterdamse
Schouwburg, Rotterdam, 1988

with the members of Nuclear Nine and H.'s boss seated at the head of the table.

The boss makes a speech urging H. to perform one last great labor for the company and its future. Although M. and her children do all that they can to dissuade H. from taking on the responsibility, he is ready to perform his duty as a company man and fight whatever evil may stand in the way of his mission.

Entr'acte. Video: "Talking Head"
Two banks of thirty-two monitors on tracks slide onto the stage from right and left. Boss's head appears on the huge screen of sixty-four monitors. He gives a speech about H.'s mission that is intercut with scenes of the boardroom, L.E.D. stock quotations, and H. suiting up like a warrior in armor and high-tech weaponry.

Solid Ashes, 1988
In performance at Rotterdamse
Schouwburg, Rotterdam, 1988

II. Into the Machine

H. finds himself in some kind of postapocalyptic crack in the earth. He is walking in a canyon of biomorphic technologial infrastructures. The action is slowed by a seemingly overwhelming gravity. The sky is of a murky brown viscosity. The canyon closes in on H., attacking him. The battle becomes increasingly barbaric and savage. Whereas first H. overcomes his adversaries with wit and intelligence, he later strips himself of all technological means, drawing blood and fighting solely with primitive anger.

He succeeds but is visibly drained by the physical violence.

Entr'acte. Video: "Landscapes"
In a series of virgin landscapes, one dissolving into another, a woman recites Heiner Müller's story, "Hercules and the Hydra II." She appears and

reappears in different parts of the fields and skies but continues to recite the story with a mesmerizing, powerful cadence in her voice. She stands as a self-contained statue.

Woman: For a long time he still believed he would pass through the forest in the narcotically warm wind, which seemed to blow from all sides and which moved the trees like snakes, in the constant twilight of barely visible tracks of blood on the continually quaking ground, alone in battle with the beast. In the first days and nights—or were they only hours? How could he measure time without the sky—he still often asked himself what could lie under the ground, which swelled under his steps so that it seemed to breathe, how thin was the skin over the unknown below and how long would it hold him up out of the bowels of the earth? . . .

Solid Ashes, 1988
In performance at Rotterdamse
Schouwburg, Rotterdam, 1988

He threw himself forward out of the embrace in a sudden spurt. He knew he had never run faster. He didn't gain a step—the forest kept pace; he stayed in its clutches, which now closed in on him and squeezed his bowels together. How long could he stand the pressure? Then he understood, in his rising panic: the forest was the beast, the forest which he had thought he was passing through had become the beast a long time before. It was carrying him in the tempo of its steps, the groundswells its breaths, the wind its breathing, the track he had been following his own blood, which the forest that was the beast, for how long, how much blood did a man have, had been sampling; he had known it all along, only not with names.

III. Coming Home

H. struggles to make his way back to the world of Nuclear Nine. He is distrustful of all that surrounds him and finds that he has returned to a different world. As he watches from above, suspended in a triangular "corridor," the scene seems to be that of his own memorial service. Gathered around the newly unveiled monument to H. are the Chairman of the Board, and H.'s wife, children, and friends, who speak of him lovingly, mournfully. A newscaster covers the event by attempting to interview people.

The lights change abruptly from the simple to chaotic. Long, dramatic shadows are cast Hitchcock-like, creating fear. The crowd responds in sync with the mood of the light. H. is confused by what he sees; he thinks that

Solid Ashes, 1988
In performance at Rotterdamse
Schouwburg, Rotterdam, 1988

168

his wife and the Chairman have become lovers. H. triggers an alarm. A siren sounds. He is then discovered by the crowd.

Entr'acte. Video: "Objects"
The scene begins with still images of perfect food, such as tomatoes, cucumbers, and eggs. Gradually we see a blade skillfully chopping and preparing food. The cutting goes faster and faster. The foods being cut become increasingly more graphic. Animals are slaughtered, meat is cut from bones, and so on. The final shot is that of a bountifully set dining table for a homecoming.

IV. The Killing

In a floating, white room, we find H. in the kitchen of his house. His family is seated at a dining table on which an elaborate festive dinner has been served. The house does not look the same to H. He acts as though he were there for the first time. H. moves silently, tentatively encircling his family; he seems to see them as enemies. No one dares to move except the youngest child. M. senses what is about to happen and tries in vain to stop him. H. cannot be stopped. He kills his children with brutal force, and finally, his wife, all with astonishing precision. All is still for a moment—then the back wall of the kitchen begins to bleed. A veil of liquid red seeps down the wall. H. has no idea what he has done.

Entr'acte. Video: "Eyewitness"
A brash newscaster interviews an eyewitness to the nightmarish scene. H.'s boss makes an official statement. While the first is improvised, emotional, and committed, the second is cool, detached, and essentially untrue.

V. Ashes

Years later we rejoin H. in an ecologically devastated landscape. It is a desert of cracked stone at the edge of a quarry; the stage is covered with water. H. wanders on from stage left barefoot and in rags. He is inconsolable. He is finally aware of what he has done and unable to find peace. A young girl plays in the water among the stones, acting as though it were just another sunny day at the beach. H.'s movements become more spasmodic and frantic. He mumbles, trying to sum up in words what his life has been reduced to.

H. sees the girl and begins to play with her. He kneels beside her in the shallow water and slowly begins to cover himself with stones as he lies face-down in the water. The girl playfully helps to cover him completely with rocks until he has become a stone grave in the water.

Curtain closes.

Edited by Jennifer Cox and Paul Gallis

Portrait of the artist, 1987

CHRONOLOGY

1953

Born in Brooklyn, New York, the youngest of three children, to Samuel and Nell Longo.

1954

Family moves to Long Island, New York.

1970

Graduates from Plainview High School and enrolls at North Texas State University in Denton.

1971

Leaves North Texas State. Buys a Volkswagen van and drives around the U.S. on his way to New York; stops at Gettysburg, Pennsylvania, site of the Civil War battle. The Civil War has fascinated Longo since boyhood and its images would appear in his art years later.

1972

Enters night school at Nassau Community College on Long Island; during the day works in a warehouse and then for an industrial designer in New York City; begins going to museums. Takes art classes with the sculptor Leonda Finke, who encourages him to pursue his creative interests. Receives a grant to study art history and painting restoration at the Accademia di Belle Arti in Florence.

1973

Arrives in Milan where he sees Leonardo da Vinci's *Last Supper* and modern Italian art, including Boc-

cioni's futurist sculpture. At the Accademia he assists conservators who are restoring art damaged in the flood of 1966. Frustrated with the slow pace of the work, he leaves to travel through Italy, Spain, and France and see art history at first hand. He ends his tour in Paris, where the Rodin Museum particularly affects him; the experience convinces him that he wants to be an artist.

Fall: Back in New York, enters art school at the State University College in Buffalo. Discovers the Albright-Knox Art Gallery. Meets two young art students, Philip Malkin and Richard Zucker, who share his intense curiosity about art; they read art magazines, discuss art, and experiment with various mediums. Gets acquainted with the Media Center at the State University of New York in Buffalo, where the filmmakers Hollis Frampton and Paul Sharits are working. Assists Sharits in making films and drawings. At the Media Center sees the film *La Jetée* (1963), by Chris Marker, which makes a great impression on Longo and influences his later work, particularly the Men in the Cities series.

1974

Summer: Meets Cindy Sherman; they go on "art dates" to museums. Sherman joins the team of Longo, Malkin, and Zucker; the four invent a student whom they enroll in school with them and call Rose Scaleci; like Marcel Duchamp's Rose Selavy, she becomes their alter ego. With Professor Joseph Piccillo's encouragement, they arrange exhibitions at the school of their own work and others.

Meets Charles Clough, who lives in an old abandoned ice factory, converted by the Ashford Hollow

The artist and friends in Buffalo, c. 1975. From left to right: Philip Malkin (front), Joseph Hryvniak (hand on knee), Joseph Panone, the artist, Charles Clough, Kevin Noble, Richard Zucker, Judy Treible, Gary Judkins, Linda Cathcart, George Howell, Michael Zwack, Larry Lundy, Cindy Sherman, unidentified woman

Announcement card, Gallery 229, Buffalo, New York, 1975

The artist's studio at the Ashford Hollow Foundation, Buffalo, New York, c. 1975

Foundation into studio space for artists. Longo and Sherman move into an apartment nearby, and Longo gets a studio at the foundation, across from Clough, whose range of knowledge about art Longo finds inspiring and instructive; together with Clough, Michael Zwack, and others, starts Hallwalls—an exhibition space in the hall between their studios. Funded by Jack Griffith, codirectors Longo and Clough begin to invite New York City artists they have been reading about to come up to Buffalo.

Experiments with performance, installations, and video. He is influenced by the art of Bruce Nauman, Robert Smithson, and Robert Irwin, who visits Buffalo and encourages Longo and the other artists in their plans for Hallwalls.

February: First Hallwalls exhibition, *Working on Paper,* including seventy-five artists from Buffalo and other cities, is organized by Longo and Clough.

1975

Meets Linda Cathcart, newly appointed curator at the Albright-Knox Art Gallery, who lends support to the Hallwalls group. Hallwalls flourishes through grants from the New York State Council on the Arts and National Endowment for the Arts. On trips to New York, Clough and Longo invite artists and art critics to Buffalo. Among them, Vito Acconci, John Baldessari, Lizzie Borden, Joan Jonas, Sol LeWitt, Lucy Lippard, Judy Pfaff, Richard Serra, and Michael Snow visit, exhibit, lecture, or set up installations.

1976

January: Stages first performance piece, *Artful Dodger,* at Hallwalls and then, in April, in Montreal

Temptation to Exit, 1976, in performance at Artists Space, New York, 1976

The artist with *Seven Seals for Missouri Breaks* in the Ashford Hollow foundry, c.1976, Buffalo, New York

at Véhicule Art. Meets Helene Winer, director of Artists Space, New York; at her invitation, in October does a performance there called *Temptation to Exit/ Things I Will Regret*; the performance involves a number of Longo's friends from Buffalo and is an early demonstration of his predilection for collaboration. While in New York, sees a show by Jonathan Borofsky at Paula Cooper Gallery. Invites Borofsky to Hallwalls, where he gets snowed in for ten days. After this unexpectedly long and intense encounter, Longo makes his first reliefs with clay that Borofsky leaves in his studio.

Through Winer, meets recent graduates of California Institute of the Arts—Jack Goldstein, Troy Brauntuch, David Salle, Matt Mullican, and Paul McMahon—and later (in 1977) organizes a group exhibition of their work as his final show at Hallwalls.

March: Longo's relief *Seven Seals for Missouri Breaks* (1976) is included in exhibition *In Western New York*, directed by Douglas Schultz and Linda Cathcart, at Albright-Knox Art Gallery; Winer and art critic Douglas Crimp attend the opening and ask Longo to take part in an upcoming exhibition, *Pictures*, at Artists Space.

Summer: Moves with Sherman to New York; they sublet an apartment from Brauntuch on Fulton Street; Crimp, Salle, and artist-critic Tom Lawson all live nearby. Longo and Sherman later move into a loft on South Street, also nearby.

Works as an assistant to Acconci; does construction work and paints lofts with Zwack, who, with artist Nancy Dwyer, had also moved to New York from Buffalo. Frequents Bleecker Street Cinema; the films of Francis Ford Coppola, Jean-Luc Godard, Rainer Werner Fassbinder, and Martin Scorsese make a particularly strong impression on him. Goes to the Mudd Club, CBGB, Tier 3, and Hurrahs, where he becomes involved with the downtown New York music scene.

Makes the relief *The American Soldier* (titled after the Fassbinder film); it is an image that will reappear in the Men in the Cities drawings.

September: Opening of *Pictures*, a group exhibition, at Artists Space; the young artists in this show—Brauntuch, Jack Goldstein, Sherrie Levine, Longo, and Philip Smith—believe it will be a turning point in their careers and hold great hopes for it.

1978

Loft on South Street is under vacate orders; lives with utilities turned off. German curator and art historian Kasper König visits the studio and offers Longo some much-needed financial assistance to continue his work.

Takes over temporarily for Carlotta Schoolman, curator of exhibitions, video, and performance at The Kitchen. Working with performance artists Eric Bogosian and Jill Kroesen and composers Rhys Chatham and Joseph Hannan, he brings in a new wave of artists. Arranges exhibitions of Salle, Brauntuch, Goldstein, Acconci, and performances by bands such as Theoretical Girls. Using backdrop paper brought home from The Kitchen, Longo makes untitled black-and-white figure drawings of a cowboy and a

Cover of *Sun & Moon: A Journal of Literature and Art,* 1979

Percival Completed, 1979. Graphite and acrylic on canvas. 84 × 96 in. (213 × 244 cm). Collection of the Chase Manhattan Bank

puncher, the former inspired by Andy Warhol's film *Lonesome Cowboy* (1968) and the latter, by Henri Clouzot's *Wages of Fear* (1953).

Meets Janelle Reiring, who is directing an exhibition with Sherman's Untitled Film Stills at Artists Space.

1979

Howard N. Fox, then a curator at the Hirshhorn Museum and Sculpture Garden in Washington, D.C., writes the first article on Longo's work for *Sun and Moon: A Journal of Literature and Art* (published Fall 1979).

Meets Diane Shea, a professional illustrator, who is hired to work on the oversize drawing *Percival Completed* (seven by eight feet); Shea remains Longo's most important collaborator to this day.

April: *Boys Slow Dance,* Longo's first solo exhibition in New York, opens at The Kitchen; organized by RoseLee Goldberg, it includes a series of cast-aluminum reliefs—*The Wrestlers, Swing,* and *The Pilots* (all 1978)—and a performance called *Surrender,* with musician Peter Gordon.

Over his head in debt, Longo drives a taxi at night for several months. Continues to make large-scale black-

The artist's South Street studio, c. 1979

The artist (far right) performing with Rhys Chatham Band, c. 1982

The artist (second from right) performing with Menthol Wars, 1980

and-white drawings, first projecting figures from magazine illustrations and then from photographs of friends—first two, Bogosian and Hannan. Begins to play guitar in bands: Morales, Rhys Chatham Band, Menthol Wars (with Richard Prince, Hannan, Jeffrey Glenn, and David Linton), Built on Guilt, Bang Electric Speak (with Zwack and Hannan).

Triptych, *Men Trapped in Ice* (1979), is included in a group show at the Max Protetch Gallery, New York, the first commercial gallery to show Longo's work.

1980

January: Takes part in the exhibition *Extensions: Jennifer Bartlett, Lynda Benglis, Robert Longo, and Judy Pfaff* at the Contemporary Arts Museum in Houston, organized by Linda Cathcart, then director of the museum. Meets the art dealer Brooke Alexander, who

invites him to participate in the exhibition *Illustration and Allegory* (May) at his gallery in New York and becomes Longo's first print publisher; meets Carter Ratcliff through the exhibition.

February: Performance of *Surrender* at D.C. Space in Washington, D.C.; while there, lectures at The Corcoran Gallery of Art. Also meets artist Gretchen Bender, who later moves in with Longo and becomes the first female subject for Men in the Cities series.

Begins working with Domenico Ranieri Sculpture Casting, with whom he continues to work to this day.

June: First European one-man show, at Studio d'Arte Cannaviello, Milan; travels in Italy with Troy Brauntuch.

October: Goes on a European performance tour organized by The Kitchen with Bogosian, Hannan, Chatham, dancer Molissa Fenley, composer Jeffry Lohn, and choreographers and dancers Bill T. Jones and Arnie Zane, who become Bender and Longo's close friends and collaborators.

November: Helene Winer and Janelle Reiring open Metro Pictures, a commercial gallery in New York. Longo participates in opening exhibition.

1981

January: First solo New York gallery exhibition, at Metro Pictures, includes six nine-foot Men in the Cities drawings. Establishes precedent of crediting his assistants/collaborators/fabricators, listing their names on the wall of the gallery.

Set for *Intuitive Momentum,* in performance at the Brooklyn Academy of Music, New York, 1982

Directs *Fictive Victims,* an exhibition of younger artists (including Mark Innerst, Bill Komoski, Jim Isermann, and Anne Doran) at Hallwalls in Buffalo.

March: Appears on the cover of *Arts* magazine.

April: Stages performances of *Empire* trilogy at The Corcoran Gallery of Art, Washington, D.C.

May: König includes Longo in *Westkunst* exhibition in Cologne.

June: Men in the Cities series featured in one-man show at Larry Gagosian Gallery, Los Angeles; meets novelist Richard Price, who will later write the screenplay for *Steel Angels* (a film project still uncompleted) from Longo's storyboards. Meets composer David Byrne, whose figure Longo later incorporates into his combine *Heads Will Roll* (1984).

Designs album cover for Ascension by Glenn Branca for 99 Records.

1982

February: Two-person show with Cindy Sherman at Texas Gallery, Houston, where he meets Walter Hopps, director of the Menil Collection, Houston.

Buys first of several color television sets for his studio.

April: Three large cropped Men in the Cities drawings shown at the Whitney Museum of American Art, New York, in *Focus on the Figure: Twenty Years.*

The combine *National Trust* (1981) is acquired by the Walker Art Center, Minneapolis.

Designs sets for musician Max Roach and dancers Bill

T. Jones and Arnie Zane and Company performance called *Intuitive Momentum* at the Brooklyn Academy of Music.

June: Invited to participate in *Documenta 7* in Kassel, West Germany, shows *Corporate Wars: Walls of Influence* (1982).

Meets critic Hal Foster, who is writing "The Art of Spectacle" for *Art in America* on Longo's work.

1983

February: Joint exhibition at Leo Castelli and Metro Pictures. Kynaston McShine, curator at The Museum of Modern Art, New York, sees preview of the new combine pieces in the show and initiates the acquisition of *Pressure* (1982–83).

March: Included in the Whitney Museum of American Art *1983 Biennial Exhibition.* Publishes first lithographs with Brooke Alexander, printed by Maurice Sanchez, in New York.

Sword of the Pig (1983) is acquired by the Tate Gallery, London. Publishes prints with Jorg Schellmann, and exhibits at Schellmann and Bernd Klüser's gallery in Munich (June); while there, meets actors and crew who worked with Fassbinder; visits Nuremberg and Dachau.

1984

April: Exhibition of Men in the Cities drawings and reliefs organized by I. Michael Danoff at the Akron Art Museum, Akron, Ohio.

May: Solo exhibition at Metro Pictures consolidates Longo's shift from individual drawings and sculptures to the combine pieces. Included in the show is *Tongue to the Heart* (1984).

Begins working with composer Stuart Argabright.

Participates in the reopening exhibition, *International Survey of Recent Painting and Sculpture,* at the newly expanded Museum of Modern Art, New York.

November: Solo exhibition at the Larry Gagosian Gallery, Los Angeles; also stages performance works for Art of Spectacle series at James Corcoran Gallery Annex, Venice.

Samuel Longo dies.

Travels to Munich to work with Lothar Schirmer, who will publish monograph on Longo with text by Carter

Ratcliff (published in America by Rizzoli).

December: Directs *Forced Sentiment* at Artists Space, a show of new artists, including Kevin Larmon, Joel Otterson, and Steven Parrino.

1985

Moves studio to Centre Street in Little Italy; plays basketball regularly in nearby schoolyard with Brauntuch, Foster, artist Rick Franklin, film executive Jonathan Bender, and others.

Record album covers designed by the artist for Glenn Branca (1981) and The Replacements (1985)

April: In cooperation with solo exhibition of drawings and combines, titled *Temple of Love*, organized by Charlotta Kotik, stages performance works at The Brooklyn Museum, including premier of *Marble Fog*, which wins a Bessie (New York Dance and Performance Award).

Eric Bogosian, Jo Bonney, Tim Carr, the artist, and Gretchen Bender, Christmas, 1985

Exhibition of photographs for Men in the Cities drawings at Stedelijk Museum, Amsterdam.

Designs album cover for *Tim* by The Replacements for Sire Record Company.

May: Appears on cover of *Artnews*.

November: Takes part in *Carnegie International* at Museum of Art, Carnegie Institute, in Pittsburgh. Travels to Italy with his mother and architect Joseph Di Monda for an exhibition at the Lia Rumma Gallery, Naples; has private viewing of Caravaggio paintings at the Museo di Capodimonte and has marble work carved at Carrara; visits relatives in Sicily.

1986

Makes first music video, Golden Palominos' "Boy (Go)." Meets Michael Stipe of R.E.M.; Longo later makes a video for R.E.M. ("The One I Love," 1987), and Stipe acts in Longo's film *Arena Brains* (1987).

Summer: Longo and Bender rent a house with Cindy Sherman and video artist Michel Auder on the north shore of Long Island, near the Longo family summer house; they continue to spend summers in the same area.

Travels to Japan with Bender to arrange an upcoming exhibition and meets filmmaker Sogo Ishi.

In an especially productive period, Longo creates a large body of new sculptural combines, which appear in October in exhibitions at Metro Pictures in New York and Donald Young Gallery in Chicago; among the pieces included are *All You Zombies: Truth before God, Machines in Love,* and *Death and Taxes* (all from 1986). The Art Institute of Chicago acquires *Death and Taxes*.

The artist directing Sean Young, Richard Price, and Tom Gilroy
(seated clockwise around table) in *Arena Brains*, 1987

October: Returns to Japan for an exhibition at the Wacoal Art Center; the Lounge Lizards and John Lurie play for the opening of the show. In Japan makes *Stacked Odds,* which marks a new, nonrepresentational emphasis in his work.

Meets Bob Krasnow, chairman of Elektra/Asylum/Nonesuch Records, who agrees to produce Longo's film *Arena Brains.*

1987

June: *All You Zombies: Truth before God, Machines in Love,* and *Samurai Overdrive* (1986) are included in *Documenta 8,* Kassel, West Germany. Travels to Paris for a solo exhibition at the Galerie Daniel Templon and a survey show at the Centre Georges Pompidou, celebrating its first decade; Longo and Bender meet philosopher Paul Virilio.

September: New film, *Arena Brains,* premiers at the New York Film Festival.

October: Creates performance work *Killing Angels* to inaugurate reopening of Burchfield Art Center, State University College, Buffalo.

1988

Two solo shows—Longo and Salle—at Menil Collection, Houston, organized by Walter Hopps.

The artist with musician Vernon Reid, 1988

Installing *Robert Longo* exhibition at Metro Pictures, New York, 1988

Arnie Zane dies of AIDS.

Spring: Lectures at The Museum of Modern Art for Contemporary Art in Context series, speaking about Jackson Pollock in particular.

Summer: Returns to Gettysburg and sees reenactment of the Civil War battle, which inspires the combines *Nostromo* (1988) and *A House Divided: Re-enactor* (1988).

Meets Thomas Kellein, new director of Kunsthalle Basel; they begin plans for a 1991 solo exhibition.

October: Performances of *Solid Ashes* in Rotterdam; simultaneously creates a large installation at the Museum Boymans–van Beuningen called *Object Ghosts and Love Collectors,* using photographs from the Gettysburg reenactment.

Cindy Sherman, Bill T. Jones, Michel Auder, Linda Cathcart, Gretchen Bender, Arthur Aviles, and the artist on the beach at Malibu, 1989

1989

Winter: Contributes a statement to the catalogue of *Andy Warhol: A Retrospective* at The Museum of Modern Art, New York.

Acquires film rights to William Gibson's short story "Johnny Mnemonic." Hamburg and Longo begin writing the script.

April: Participates in a media symposium at Nippon Hoso Kyokai television network in Tokyo and travels to Osaka for the installation of *Machines in Love* (1986), recently acquired by the IMG collection.

May: Included in group show, *A Forest of Signs,* at the Museum of Contemporary Art, Los Angeles, which brings together many of the artists from the late seventies *Pictures* generation.

Fall: Linda Cathcart opens an art gallery in Santa Monica, California, and devotes first exhibition to Longo's art.

Portrait of the artist, 1988

Installation view, Leo Castelli, New York, 1983

EXHIBITION HISTORY

ONE-PERSON EXHIBITIONS

1974

Gallery 220, State University College, Buffalo, New York.

Upton Gallery, State University College, Buffalo, New York.

1975

State University College, Buffalo, New York. *Passage.* Spring.

1976

Hallwalls, Buffalo, New York. *Object Fictions: A Situation of Props.* September 24–October 6.

1979

The Kitchen, New York. *Robert Longo: Boys Slow Dance.* April 28–May 19.

1980

Studio d'Arte Cannaviello, Milan. *Robert Longo.* June.

1981

Metro Pictures, New York. *Robert Longo: Men in the Cities.* January 10–31.

Main Gallery, Fine Arts Center, University of Rhode Island, Kingston. *Men in the Cities: An Exhibition by Robert Longo.* March 4–27.

Larry Gagosian Gallery, Los Angeles. *Robert Longo.* June 16–July 18.

RAW (Real Art Ways), Hartford, Connecticut. *Silent Running.* December 4–21.

1982

Texas Gallery, Houston. *Robert Longo.* February 13–March 6.

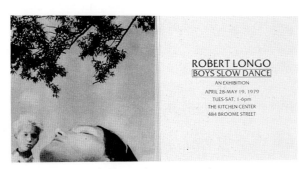

Announcement card, The Kitchen, New York, 1979

Installation view, Metro Pictures, New York, 1983

Installation view, Metro Pictures, New York, 1984

1983

Brooke Alexander, New York. *Robert Longo: Recent Lithographs, Screenprints, and Sculpture in Small Editions*. January 15–February 8.

Leo Castelli and Metro Pictures, New York (joint exhibition). *Robert Longo*. February 5–26 (Castelli), February 5–March 5 (Metro).

Galerie Schellmann und Klüser, Munich. *Robert Longo*. June 9–September 8.

1984

Akron Art Museum, Akron, Ohio. *Robert Longo: Drawings and Reliefs*. April 7–June 10. Catalogue introduction by I. Michael Danoff, essay by Hal Foster.

Metro Pictures, New York. *Robert Longo*. April 28–May 26.

Larry Gagosian Gallery, Los Angeles. *Robert Longo: Body of a Comic—Four New Works for Los Angeles*. November 8–December 1.

Installation view, Lia Rumma Gallery, Naples, 1985

1985

The Brooklyn Museum, New York. *Robert Longo: Temple of Love*. March 1–May 6.

University of Iowa Museum of Art, Iowa City. *Robert Longo: Dis-Illusions*. March 25–September 15. Catalogue essay by Robert Hobbs.

Brooke Alexander, New York. *Robert Longo: Men in the Cities: Lithographs 1982–1985*. November 9–December 7.

Lia Rumma Gallery, Naples. *Robert Longo*.

Stedelijk Museum, Amsterdam (photographs).

Installation view, *Steel Angels, Part II*, Metro Pictures, New York, 1986

1986

University Art Museum, California State University, Long Beach. *Robert Longo, Sequences: Men in the Cities*. March 18–April 20. Traveled to Contemporary Arts Museum, Houston, May 30–June 29; and Fort Wayne Museum of Art, Fort Wayne, Indiana, November 15, 1986–January 11, 1987. Catalogue essay by Lucinda Barnes.

Norman Mackenzie Art Gallery, University of Regina, Saskatchewan. *Robert Longo: Studies and Prints*. March 21–May 4. Catalogue essay by Michael Parke-Taylor.

Metro Pictures, New York. *Steel Angels, Part I*, May 3–June 14; *Steel Angels, Part II*, October 18–November 15.

Donald Young Gallery, Chicago. *Robert Longo: New Works*. October 14–November 15.

Spiral Gallery, Wacoal Art Center, Tokyo. *Longo in Tokyo*. October 24–December 28. Catalogue essay by Janju Itoh.

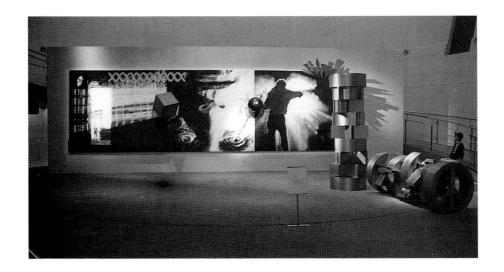

1987

Galerie Daniel Templon, Paris. *Robert Longo*. June 3–July 18.

1988

The Menil Collection, Houston. *Robert Longo*. May 21–September 4.

Metro Pictures, New York. *Robert Longo*. October 8–November 5.

Museum Boymans-van Beuningen, Rotterdam. *Robert Longo: Object Ghosts and Love Collectors*. October 8–November 20.

Above: Installation view, Wacoal Art Center, Tokyo, 1986
Below: Installation view, Museum Boymans-van Beuningen, Rotterdam, 1988

GROUP EXHIBITIONS

1975

Gallery 219, State University of New York, Buffalo. *Spatial Survey.*

Hallwalls, Buffalo, New York. *Working on Paper: Developing the Idea.* February 27–March 12.

1976

Hallwalls, Buffalo, New York. *Noise.* June 4–26.

Artists Space, New York. *Hallwalls: An Exchange Show of Artists Associated with Hallwalls, Buffalo.* November 6–27.

1977

Albright-Knox Art Gallery, Buffalo, New York. *In Western New York.* March 26–April 17. Catalogue.

Artists Space, New York. *Pictures.* September 24–October 29. Traveled to Allen Memorial Art Museum, Oberlin, Ohio, February 28–March 25, 1978; Los Angeles Institute of Contemporary Art, April 15–May 15; 1978; Fine Arts Gallery, University of Colorado Museum, Boulder, September 8–October 6, 1978. Catalogue by Douglas Crimp.

Hallwalls, Buffalo, New York. *Wherenwhen* (organized in collaboration with CEPA). December 3.

1978

N.A.M.E. Gallery, Chicago. *Buffalo / Chicago / Exchango* (exchange exhibition between Hallwalls and N.A.M.E.). September 15–October 7.

1979

Max Protetch Gallery, New York. *Re: Figuration.*

Upton Gallery, State University College, Buffalo, New York. *Hallwalls: 5 Years.* November 5–15. Traveled to A Space, Toronto, February 16–March 8, 1980; Parsons Gallery (sponsored by The New Museum), New York, June 19–July 18, 1980. Catalogue essay by Linda Cathcart.

Hal Bromm Gallery, New York. *New Talent.*

1980

Contemporary Arts Museum, Houston. *Extensions:*

Jennifer Bartlett, Lynda Benglis, Robert Longo, Judy Pfaff. January 20–March 2. Catalogue by Linda Cathcart.

Palazzo della Triennale, Milan. *XVI Triennale: Nuova Immagine.* April–July. Catalogue.

Brooke Alexander, New York. *Illustration and Allegory.* May 13–June 14. Catalogue by Carter Ratcliff.

Hal Bromm Gallery, New York. *A Matter of Choice: Selections by Critics, Artists, and Collectors.* October 4–28.

Metro Pictures, New York. *Opening Group Exhibition.* November 15–December 3.

Annina Nosei Gallery, New York. *Drawings and Paintings on Paper.* December 20–January 17.

1981

Sidney Janis Gallery, New York. *New Directions: A Corporate Collection Selected by Sam Hunter.* February 12–March 7. Catalogue by Sam Hunter.

Museo Sant'Agostino, Genoa. *Il Gergo Inquieto.* March–April.

Wave Hill, New York. *Tableaux.* May 15–October 18. Catalogue by Kim Levin.

Rheinhallen, Museen der Stadt, Cologne, West Germany. *Westkunst: Internationale Ausstellung.* May 30–August 16. Catalogue by Kasper König.

Metro Pictures, New York. *Drawings.* June 10–July 31.

Galerie Chantal Crousel, Paris. *Picturealism.* June.

Brooke Alexander, New York. *Represent, Representation, Representative.* September 8–October 3.

Paula Cooper Gallery, New York. *Tenth Anniversary Benefit for The Kitchen.* September 19–26.

Hayden Gallery, List Visual Arts Center, Massachusetts Institute of Technology, Cambridge. *Body Language: Figurative Aspects of Recent Art.* October 2–December 24. Traveled to Fort Worth Art Museum, Texas, September 11–October 24, 1982; University of Southern Florida Art Gallery, Tampa, November 12–December 17, 1982; Contemporary Arts Center, Cincinnati, January 14–February 26, 1983. Catalogue essay by Roberta Smith.

Institute for Art and Urban Resources, P.S. 1, Long

Installation view, Albright-Knox Art Gallery, Buffalo, New York, 1981

Island City, New York. *Figuratively Sculpting.* October 18–December 13.

Albright-Knox Art Gallery, Buffalo, New York. *Figures: Forms and Expressions.* November 20, 1981–January 3, 1982. Catalogue by Charlotta Kotik.

Artists Space, New York. *35 Artists Return to Artists Space.* December 3–24. Catalogue.

1982

Zabriskie Gallery, New York. *Flat and Figurative: 20th Century Wall Sculpture.* January 6–February 6.

Portland Center for the Visual Arts, Portland, Oregon. *A Few Good Men.* January 15–February 28.

Contemporary Arts Center, New Orleans. *The Human Figure in Contemporary Art.* March 5–April 4.

Contemporary Arts Center, Cincinnati. *Dynamix.* March 11–April 17. Traveled to Sullivant Hall Gallery, Ohio State University, Columbus, September 6–October 17; Allen Memorial Art Museum, Oberlin College, Oberlin, Ohio, November 1–21; Butler Institute of American Art, Youngstown, Ohio, December 6, 1982–January 9, 1983; University of Kentucky Art Museum, Lexington, January 15–February 20, 1983; Joslyn Art Museum, Omaha, March 19–May 1, 1983; Doane Hall Art Gallery, Allegheny College, Meadville, Pennsylvania, May 5–27, 1983. Catalogue essay by Robert Sterns.

University Art Gallery, San Diego State University, La

Jolla, California. *Body Language: A Notebook of Contemporary Figuration.* March 13–April 10.

University Fine Arts Galleries and School of Visual Arts, Florida State University, Tallahassee. *New New York.* March 17–April 17. Traveled to Metropolitan Museum and Art Centers, Coral Gables. July 9–August 30. Catalogue by Albert Stewart.

Georgia State University Art Gallery, Atlanta. *Figurative Images: Aspects of Recent Art.* April 1–May 5.

Pratt Institute (Manhattan), New York. *Tracking, Tracing, Marking, Pacing.* April 3–May 8. Traveled to Pratt Institute (Brooklyn), New York. September 29–October 26. Catalogue by Ellen Schwartz.

School of Visual Arts Museum, New York. *The New Reliefs.* April 5–23.

Whitney Museum of American Art, New York. *Focus on the Figure: Twenty Years.* April 15–June 13. Catalogue by Barbara Haskell.

Walker Art Center, Minneapolis. *Eight Artists: The Anxious Edge.* April 25–June 13. Catalogue by Lisa Lyons.

The Renaissance Society at the University of Chicago. *A Fatal Attraction: Art and the Media.* May 2–June 12. Catalogue by Thomas Lawson.

Whitney Museum of American Art, Downtown Branch, New York. *Frames of Reference.* May 6–June 4. Catalogue.

Neue Galerie, Kassel, West Germany. *Documenta 7*. June 19–September 28. Catalogue essay by Paul Dieruch.

Indianapolis Museum of Art, Indianapolis, Indiana. *Painting and Sculpture Today*. July 6–August 15. Catalogue essays by Helen Ferrulli and Robert Yassin.

Sidney Janis Gallery, New York. *The Expressionist Image: American Art from Pollock to Today*. October 9–30.

Institute of Contemporary Arts, London. *Urban Kisses*. October 14–December 28. Catalogue: *Brand New York*: Special Issue of *A Literary Review*. Essays by Iwona Blazwick, Hal Foster, Rosalind Krauss, et al.

Institute of Contemporary Art, Boston. *Art and Dance: Images of the Modern Dialogue, 1890–1980*. November 9, 1982–January 8, 1983. Traveled to Toledo Museum of Art, March 6–April 24, 1983; Neuberger Museum, State University of New York, Purchase, June 26–September 25, 1983. Catalogue.

Milwaukee Art Museum. *New Figuration in America*. December 3, 1982–January 23, 1983. Catalogue essays by Russell Bowman and Peter Schjeldahl.

Institute of Contemporary Art, University of Pennsylvania, Philadelphia. *Image Scavengers: Painting*. December 8, 1982–January 30, 1983. Catalogue by Janet Kardon.

Artists Space, New York. *Hundreds of Drawings*. December 10, 1982–January 14, 1983.

1983

University Art Museum, University of California, Santa Barbara. *A Heritage Renewed: Representational Drawing Today*. March 2–April 17. Traveled to Oklahoma Art Center, Oklahoma City, June 26–August 7; Elvehjem Museum of Art, University of Wisconsin, Madison, August 21–October 19; Colorado Springs Fine Arts Center, Colorado Springs, Colorado, November 5–December 18. Catalogue essays by Phyllis Plous and Eileen Guggenheim.

School of Visual Arts Museum, New York. *Big American Figure Drawing*. March 7–24.

Daniel Weinberg Gallery, Los Angeles. *Drawing Conclusions*. March 9–April 9.

Hirshhorn Museum and Sculpture Garden, Smithsonian Institution, Washington, D.C. *Directions 1983*. March 10–May 15. Catalogue by Phyllis Rosenzweig.

Whitney Museum of American Art, New York. *1983 Biennial Exhibition*. March 15–May 22. Catalogue.

The Renaissance Society at the University of Chicago. *The Sixth Day: A Survey of Recent Developments in Figurative Sculpture*. May 8–June 15. Catalogue by Richard Flood.

Kunstmuseum, Lucerne. *Back to the U.S.A.* May 29–July 31. Traveled to Rheinisches Landesmuseum, Bonn, West Germany; Württembergischer Kunstverein, Stuttgart. Catalogue by Klaus Honnef.

Leo Castelli, New York. *Drawings / Photographs*. Summer.

Tate Gallery, London. *New Art at the Tate Gallery 1983*. September 14–October 23. Catalogue by Michael Compton.

Stedelijk van Abbemuseum, Eindhoven, the Netherlands. *Walter Dahn, Rene Daniels, Isa Genzken, Jenny Holzer, Robert Longo, Henk Visch*. October 10–November 20. Catalogue by R. H. Fuchs.

Museum of Fine Arts, Boston. *Brave New Works: Recent American Painting and Drawings*. November 10, 1983–January 29, 1984.

Bonner Kunstverein, Bonn, West Germany. *Ansatzpunkte kritischer Kunst heute*. December 10, 1983–January 29, 1984.

1984

Art Gallery of New South Wales, Sydney. *The Fifth Biennale of Sydney, Private Symbol: Social Metaphor*. April 11–June 17. Catalogue essay by Carter Ratcliff.

Hunter College Art Gallery, New York. *Endgame: Strategies of Postmodernist Performance*. May 16–June 20. Catalogue by Maurice Berger.

The Museum of Modern Art, New York. *An International Survey of Recent Painting and Sculpture*. May 17–August 19. Catalogue.

Artists Space, New York. *A Decade of New Art*. May 31–June 30. Catalogue.

San Francisco Museum of Modern Art. *The Human Condition: SFMMA Biennial III*. June 28–August 26. Catalogue essays by Dorothy Martinson, Wolfgang

Marfaust, Achille Bonito Oliva, Klaus Ottmann, and Edward Kienholz.

Musée National d'Art Moderne, Centre National d'Art et de Culture Georges Pompidou, Paris. *Alibis*. July 5–September 17. Catalogue.

Museum of Contemporary Art, Los Angeles. *Automobile and Culture*. July 21, 1984–January 6, 1985. Traveled to Detroit Institute of Arts, June 9, 1985–September 9, 1986. Catalogue.

Institute of Contemporary Art, Boston. *Currents*. September 6–November 5. Catalogue by Elizabeth Sussman.

Contemporary Arts Center, Cincinnati. *Disarming Images: Art for Nuclear Disarmament*. September 14–October 27. Traveled to University Art Gallery, San Diego State University; Museum of Art, Washington State University, Pullman; New York State University Museum, Albany; University Art Museum, University of California, Santa Barbara; Munson-Williams-Proctor Institute Museum of Art, Utica, New York; Fine Arts Gallery, University of Nevada, Las Vegas; Baxter Art Gallery, California Institute of Technology, Pasadena; Yellowstone Art Center, Billings, Montana; Bronx Museum of the Arts, New York. End of tour: November 20, 1986. Catalogue by Nina Felshin.

Contemporary Arts Museum, Houston. *The Heroic Figure*. September 15–November 4, 1984. Traveled to Museu Nacional de Belas Artes, Rio de Janeiro, Brazil, January 17–February 26, 1984; Museo Nacional de Bellas Artes, Santiago, Chile, April 3–May 16, 1984; Memphis Brooks Museum of Art, Memphis, Tennessee, November 17, 1984–January 6, 1985; Alexandria Museum and Visual Arts Center, Alexandria, Louisiana, February 2–March 10, 1985; Santa Barbara Museum of Art, Santa Barbara, California, April 12–June 9, 1985. Catalogue essays by Linda Cathcart and Craig Owens.

Hirshhorn Museum and Sculpture Garden, Smithsonian Institution, Washington, D.C. *Content: A Contemporary Focus, 1974–1984*. October 4, 1984–January 6, 1985. Catalogue essays by Howard N. Fox, Miranda McClintic, and Phyllis Rosenzweig.

Museo Rufino Tamayo, Mexico City. *La Narrativa Internacional de Hoy*. October 30, 1984–January 2, 1985. Traveled to Institute for Art and Urban Resources, P.S. 1, New York. Catalogue.

Rheinhallen, Art Fair, Cologne, West Germany. *Szene New York*. November 15–21. Catalogue essay by Klaus Honnef.

1985

Laguna Gloria Art Museum, Austin. *Figure It Out: Exploring the Figure in Contemporary Art*. February 16–April 8.

ARCA, Centre d'Art Contemporain, Marseilles. *New York 85*. Summer.

Galleria d'Arte Moderna, Bologna, Italy. *Anniottanta*. July 4–September 30. Catalogue essays by Renato Barilli, Flavio Caroli, Concetto Pozzati, Daniel Abadie, Lynne Cooke, Zdenek Felix, and Thomas Sokolowski.

Contemporary Arts Center, Cincinnati. *Body and Soul: Aspects of Recent Figurative Sculpture*. September 6–October 12. Catalogue essay by Sarah Rogers-Lafferty.

Whitney Museum of American Art at Philip Morris, New York. *Modern Machines: Recent Kinetic Sculpture*. October 11–December 5.

Museum of Art, Carnegie Institute, Pittsburgh. *Carnegie International*. November 9, 1985–January 5, 1986. Catalogue.

Musée d'Art Contemporain, Montreal. *Ecrans Politiques*. November 17, 1985–January 12, 1986.

Laforet Museum, Tokyo. *New York Now: Correspondences*. December 5, 1985–January 5, 1986. Traveled to Tochigi Prefectural Museum of Fine Arts, Tochigi, Japan, February 8–March 23, 1986; Tazaki Hall Espace Media, Kobe, April 4–May 10, 1986.

1986

Museum of Art, Fort Lauderdale, Florida. *An American Renaissance in Art: Painting and Sculpture since 1940*. January 17–March 30. Catalogue by Sam Hunter.

The Art Institute of Chicago. *The American Exhibition*. March 8–April 27.

Städtische Galerie im Lenbachhaus, Munich. *Hommage à Beuys*. July 16–September 28.

Haus der Kunst, Munich. *Das Automobil in der Kunst, 1886–1986*. August 9–October 5. Catalogue.

Queens Museum, New York. *Television's Impact on Contemporary Art.* September 13–October 26.

The Brooklyn Museum, New York. *Monumental Drawing: Works by 22 Contemporary Americans.* September 19–November 10. Catalogue by Charlotta Kotik.

1987

Los Angeles County Museum of Art. *Avant-Garde in the Eighties.* April 23–July 12. Catalogue by Howard N. Fox.

Musée National d'Art Moderne, Centre National d'Art et de Culture Georges Pompidou, Paris. *L'Epoque, la mode, la morale, la passion, 1977–1987.* May 21–August 17. Catalogue essays by Bernard Blistène, Catherine David, and Alfred Pacquement.

The Aldrich Museum of Contemporary Art, Ridgefield, Connecticut. *Post-Abstract Abstraction.* May 31–September 6. Catalogue.

Metro Pictures, New York. *Art against AIDS.* Opened June 4.

Kassel, West Germany. *Documenta 8.* June 12–September 20. Catalogue.

Moderna Museet, Stockholm. *Implosion: A Postmodern Perspective.* October 24, 1987–January 10, 1988. Catalogue essay by Lars Nittve, Germano Celant, Kate Linker, and Craig Owens.

Blum Art Institute, Bard College, Annandale-on-Hudson, New York. *Process and Product: The Making of Eight Contemporary Masterworks.* November 20, 1987–March 31, 1988. Catalogue introduction by Linda Weintraub, essay by Donald Kuspit.

1988

Kent Fine Arts, New York. *Altered States.* April 14–May 14. Catalogue.

Marlborough Gallery, New York. *Visions / Revisions: Contemporary Representation.* April 29–May 28. Catalogue essay by Sam Hunter.

Milwaukee Art Museum. *1988: The World of Art Today.* May 6–August 28. Catalogue by Russell Bowman.

Kresge Art Museum, Michigan State University, East Lansing. *Art of the 1980s: Artists from the Eli Broad Family Foundation Collection.* November 6–December 16. Traveled to Kalamazoo Institute of Arts, Kalamazoo, Michigan, January 6–February 19, 1989.

Bonnefantenmuseum, Maastricht, the Netherlands. *The Postmodern Explained to Children.* November 19, 1988–February 3, 1989.

Museum of Contemporary Art, Chicago. *Three Decades: The Oliver-Hoffmann Collection.* December 17, 1988–February 5, 1989.

L'Institut Néerlandais, Paris. *Concept et imagination.*

Tochigi Prefectural Museum of Fine Arts, Tochigi, Japan. *American Art since 1945.* Catalogue.

1989

Museum of Contemporary Art, Los Angeles. *A Forest of Signs: Art in the Crisis of Representation.* May 7–August 13. Catalogue essays by Ann Goldstein, Mary Jane Jacob, Howard Singerman, and Anne Rorimer.

PERFORMANCES

1975

Wilson Arts Festival, Wilson, New York. *Art Attacks.* May 24.

State University College, Buffalo, New York. *Art Attacks.* November 17.

Hallwalls, Buffalo, New York. *Rose Scaleci Presents Three-Ring Circus.* April 21–May 2. Performance of *A Living Room Environment / Installation,* with Philip Malkin and Richard Zucker.

1976

Hallwalls, Buffalo, New York. *Artful Dodger.* January 7.

Véhicule Art, Montreal, Quebec. *Robert Longo: Artful Dodger, an Episodic Strategem; L'Espace comme fiction.* April 26.

Visual Studies Workshop, Rochester, New York. *The Water in the Bucket / The Cloud in the Sky.* May 14.

Albright-Knox Art Gallery (in collaboration with Hallwalls and Delaware Park), Buffalo, New York. *Convergence and Dispersal.* June 12, 13.

Artful Dodger, 1976, in performance at Hallwalls, Buffalo, New York, 1976

Artists Space, New York. *Temptation to Exit / Things I Will Regret.* October 17.

1978

Franklin Furnace Archives, New York. *Sound Distance of a Good Man.* April 18.

Announcement card, Franklin Furnace Archives, 1978

1979

The Mudd Club, New York. *Pictures for Music* (slide projections), with Guitar Trio by Rhys Chatham. February.

The Kitchen, New York. *Robert Longo: Boys Slow Dance* (exhibition). April 28–May 19. Performance of *Surrender* (date unknown). In 1980, *Surrender* also performed at Moderna Museet, Stockholm; Amerika Haus, West Berlin; American Center, Paris; and Stedelijk van Abbemuseum, Eindhoven, the Netherlands, in a tour of performance art organized by The Kitchen.

The Kitchen, New York. *New Music, New York: A Festival of Composers and Their Music.* Performance of *Pictures for Music* (slide projections), with Guitar Trio by Rhys Chatham. June 16.

1980

D.C. Space, Washington, D.C. *Surrender.* February.

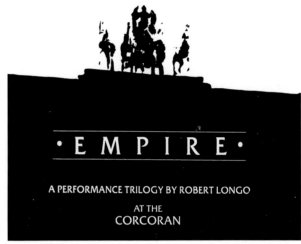

Announcement card, The Corcoran Gallery of Art, Washington, D.C., 1981

1981

The Corcoran Gallery of Art, Washington, D.C. *Empire: A Performance Trilogy.* April 15, 16.

1982

The Kitchen, New York. *Sound Distance of a Good Man, Parts I & II,* and *Iron Voices.*

1984

James Corcorcan Gallery Annex, Venice, California. *Art of Spectacle.* Performance of *Sound Distance of a Good Man* and *Surrender.* Produced by Los Angeles Contemporary Exhibitions. November 10.

1985

The Brooklyn Museum, New York. *Robert Longo: Performance Works 1977–1985.* Produced in cooperation with The Kitchen. Performance of *Sound Distance of a Good Man, Surrender,* and *Marble Fog.* April 13.

Artists Space, New York. *Memory Jam: A Retrospective Performance Series.* May 16–18.

1987

Rockwell Hall Theater, Burchfield Art Center, State University College, Buffalo, New York. *The Festival of Five.* Performance of *Killing Angels.* October 16.

1988

Rotterdamse Schouwburg, Rotterdam. *Solid Ashes,* collaborative project with Janine Brogt and Paul Gallis. October 17–26. Accompanied installation at Museum Boymans-van Beuningen, Rotterdam, *Object Ghosts and Love Collectors.* October 8–November 20.

VIDEO AND FILM PRESENTATIONS

1976

Anthology Film Archive, New York. *Experimental Video from Buffalo.* Presented *Temptation to Exit / Things I Will Regret* (video). December 25, 26.

1987

New York Film Festival. *Arena Brains* (film). September 30, October 4. 32 minutes.

Museum of Contemporary Art. Los Angeles, and Stedelijk Museum, Amsterdam (coorganizers). *The Arts for Television.* Presented "Bizarre Love Triangle" (music video). October 6–November 15 (MoCA), September 4–October 18 (Stedelijk). Catalogue essays by Kathy Rae Hoffman, Doreen Mignon, Anne

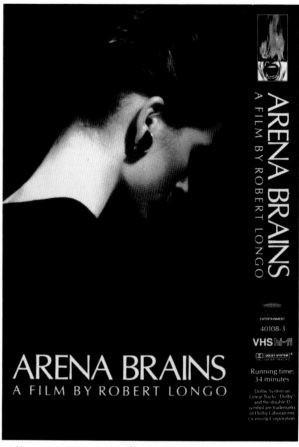

Video cover, *Arena Brains* (film), 1987

Marie Du Guet, Janet Sternberg, Ernie Tee, Rosetta Brooks, and Bob Riley.

1989

The Kitchen, New York. Music videos and the film *Arena Brains.* January 17.

BIBLIOGRAPHY

References to exhibition catalogues appear in the Exhibition History.

MONOGRAPHS

Longo, Robert. *Men in the Cities, 1979–1982.* Introduction and interview by Richard Price. New York: Harry N. Abrams, 1986.

———. *Robert Longo: Talking about "The Sword of the Pig."* London: The Tate Gallery, Patrons of New Art, 1984.

Ratcliff, Carter. *Robert Longo.* New York: Rizzoli, 1985; Munich: Schirmer/Mosel, 1985.

BOOKS

Arnason, H. H. *History of Modern Art,* 3d ed. Revised by Daniel Wheeler. New York: Harry N. Abrams, 1986.

Barber, Bruce, ed. *Performance Text(e)s & Documents,* Montreal: Boulanger, 1981.

Battcock, Gregory, ed. *The Art of Performance: A Critical Anthology.* New York: E. P. Dutton, 1984.

Celant, Germano. *Unexpressionism: Art beyond the Contemporary.* New York: Rizzoli, 1988; Genoa: Costa and Nolan, 1981.

Foster, Hal. *Recodings: Art, Spectacle, Cultural Politics.* Port Townsend, Washington: Bay Press, 1985.

Godfrey, Tony. *The New Image: Paintings in the 1980s.* New York: Abbeville Press, 1986.

Goldberg, RoseLee. *Performance: Live Art 1909 to the Present.* New York: Harry N. Abrams, 1979.

Hertz, Richard. *Theories of Contemporary Art.* Englewood Cliffs, New Jersey: Prentice-Hall, 1985.

Lee, Marshall, ed. *Art at Work: The Chase Manhattan Collection.* New York: E. P. Dutton, 1984.

Marshall, Richard. *50 New York Artists.* San Francisco: Chronicle, 1986.

New Art. Edited by Phyllis Freeman et al. New York: Harry N. Abrams, 1984.

Nordström, Gert Z. *Bilden i det Postmoderna Samhället.* Stockholm: Carlssons Bokförlag, 1989.

Oliva, Achille Bonito. *Trans Avant Garde International.* Milan: Politi, 1982.

Rosenthal, Mark. In *Art of Our Time: The Saatchi Collection,* vol. 4. New York: Rizzoli, 1984.

Wallis, Brian, ed. *Art after Modernism: Rethinking Representation.* Boston and New York: David R. Godine and The New Museum of Contemporary Art, 1984.

ARTICLES

Aletti, Vince. "Shooting Stars." *The Village Voice* (New York), 18 November 1986.

Armstrong, Richard. "Reviews: Cologne, 'Heute,' Westkunst." *Artforum* (New York) 20, no. 1 (September 1981): 85–86.

Artner, Alan G. "The Return of the Human Touch: Figurative Sculpture Is Really Back in Vogue." *Chicago Tribune,* 15 May 1983.

———. "Robert Longo Tests Power's Limits." *Chicago Tribune,* 23 October 1986.

Ashbery, John. "Biennials Bloom in the Spring." *Newsweek* (New York), 18 April 1983: 93–94.

Atkins, Robert. "Robert Longo at the Corcoran Art School." *Images and Issues* (Santa Monica, California), no. 2 (Fall 1981): 74–75.

Banes, Sally. "Performance: The Long and the Short of It." *The Village Voice* (New York), 18 May 1982.

Bannon, Anthony. " 'Figures' Is Bold and Bright, but It's Not a Shocking Show." *Buffalo Evening News*, 25 November 1981.

Bell, Jane. "Biennial Directions." *Artnews* (New York) 82, no. 6 (Summer 1983): 76–82.

Benezra, Neal. "Overstated Means/Understated Meaning: Social Content in the Art of the 1980s." *Smithsonian Studies in American Art* (Washington, D.C.) 2, no. 1 (Winter 1988): 19–31.

Berger, Maurice. "The Dynamics of Power: An Interview with Robert Longo." *Arts Magazine* (New York) 59, no. 5 (January 1985): 88–89.

Berlind, Robert. "Focus on the Figure: Twenty Years at the Whitney." *Art in America* (New York) 70, no. 10 (October 1982): 133–34.

Blinderman, Barry. "Robert Longo's 'Men in the Cities': Quotes and Commentary." *Arts Magazine* (New York) 55, no. 7 (March 1981): 92–93.

Bonaventura, Paul. "Robert Longo: A Report to the Future." *Artefactum* (Antwerp), February–March 1989: 143–44.

Brenson, Michael. "Art: Apocalyptic Pop in Mixed-Media Show." *The New York Times,* 4 May 1984.

———. "Art: Robert Longo and His Steel Angels." *The New York Times,* 16 May 1986.

———. "Artists Grapple with New Realties." *The New York Times,* 15 May 1983.

———. "A Fall Art Scene That's Bristling with Energy." *The New York Times,* 7 November 1986.

———. "Is Neo Expressionism an Idea Whose Time Has Passed?" *The New York Times,* 5 January 1986: Arts and Leisure sec.

Bromberg, Craig. "Totally Style: Robert Longo." *East Village Eye* (New York), May 1985.

Brooks, Rosetta. "Robert Longo: Leo Castelli Gallery and Metro Pictures." *Artforum* (New York) 21, no. 10 (June 1983): 83–84.

Casademont, Joan. "Represent, Representation, Representative." *Artforum* (New York) 20, no. 4 (December 1981): 73–74.

Cathcart, Linda. "The Western Image in New Work: Longo, Sherman, Zwack." *Arts Quarterly* (New Orleans) 1, no. 8 (October–December 1979): 8–9.

Chadwick, Susan. "New York Artist Brings Disturbing Images at CAM." *The Houston Post,* 8 June 1986.

Chevrier, Jean François. "Le Conflit de la toile et de l'écran." *Art Press* (Paris), no. 107 (October 1986): 20–23.

Ciardi, Nives. "Robert Longo." *Domus* (Milan), no. 635 (January 1983): 69.

Cohen, Ronny. "A Survey of What, How, and Why Younger American Artists Are Drawing So Much Today." *Drawing* (New York) 3 (July–August 1981): 25–30.

Collins, Tricia, and Richard Milazzo. "Robert Longo: Static Violence." *Flash Art* (Milan), no. 112 (May 1983): 36–38.

"La Consapevolezza del Sapere." *Abitare* (Milan), no. 250 (December 1986): 104–13.

Cotton, Linda. "Artist Longo Sculpts for Post Office." *Iowa City Weekly News,* 8 July 1982.

Cotter, Holland. "Robert Longo." *Arts Magazine* (New York) 59, no. 1 (September 1984): 7.

———. "Robert Longo at Metro Pictures." *Art in America* (New York) 77, no. 3 (March 1989): 143–44.

Crimp, Douglas. "About Pictures." *Flash Art* (Milan), no. 88–89 (March–April 1979): 34–35.

———. "The Photographic Activity of Postmodernism." *October* (New York), no. 15 (Winter 1980): 91–101.

———. "Pictures." *October* (New York), no. 8 (Spring 1979): 75–88.

Crossley, Mimi. "Review Extensions." *The Houston Post,* 25 January 1980.

Currie, W. "Profile: Hallwalls, Buffalo." *Umbrella* (Glendale, California) 2 (May 1979): 53–54.

Danieli, Fidel. "Robert Longo." *Artscene* (Los Angeles) 5 (March 1986): 7–8.

Dietrich, Barbara. "Documenta 7 en Kassel." *Goya* (Madrid) 167 (May–June 1982): 319–20.

Dika, Vera. "Robert Longo: Performance into Film." *Artscribe* (London), no. 71 (June 1988): 72–76.

Dimitrijevic, Nena. "London, Urban Kisses, Institute of Contemporary Arts." *Flash Art* (Milan), no. 110, (January 1983): 66.

"Documenta 7, Ein Rundgang." *Kunstforum International (Cologne),* September–October 1982.

Drohojowska, Hunter. "The 'Spectacles' of Robert Longo." *LA Weekly* (Los Angeles), 9–15 November 1984.

Dumont, Jean. "Ecrans politiques." *Montréal*, 23 November 1985.

Eisenman, Stephen F. "Robert Longo." *Arts Magazine* (New York) 57, no. 8 (April 1983): 43.

"Empire: A Film by Robert Longo." *Museumjournaal* (Amsterdam), no. 7 (1982): 332–35.

Feaver, William. "The Shockers." *Observer* (London), 24 October 1982.

Fisher, Jean. "Reviews: Robert Longo." *Artforum* (New York) 23, no. 1 (September 1984): 116.

Foster, Hal. "The Art of Spectacle." *Art in America* (New York) 71, no. 4 (April 1983): 144–49, 195–99.

Fox, Howard N. "Desire for Pathos: The Art of Robert Longo." *Sun and Moon* (Washington D.C.), Fall 1979: 71–80.

Frank, Peter. "Pictures and Meaning." *Artweek* (Oakland, California), 29 April 1978.

Gardner, Paul. "Longo: Making Art for Brave Eyes." *Artnews* (New York) 84, no. 5 (May 1985): 56–65.

———. "When Is a Painting Finished?" *Artnews* (New York) 84, no. 9 (November 1985): 90–91.

———. "Will Success Spoil Bob and Jim, Louise and Larry?" *Artnews* (New York) 81, no. 9 (November 1981): 109.

Geng, Veronica. "Smatta Hari." *Soho Weekly News* (New York), 15 July 1981.

Giblin, Marie. "Reviews in Brief: Washington D.C., Robert Longo: Empire." *New Art Examiner* (Chicago) 8, no. 10 (June 1981): 15.

Glatt, Cara. "Sculptors Look at Human Form." *The Chicago Herald*, 25 May 1983.

Glicksman, Marlaine. "Bravo Longo." *Film Comment* (New York) 25, no. 2 (March–April 1989): 42–46.

Glueck, Grace. "Art: Works by Longo on View at Two Galleries." *The New York Times*, 11 February 1983.

———. "Artists Who 'Scavenge' from the Media." *The New York Times*, 9 January 1983.

———. "Big American Figure Drawings." *The New York Times*, 18 March 1983.

———. "The Very Timely Art of Robert Longo." *The New York Times*, 10 March 1985.

Goldberg, RoseLee. "Performance Art for All?" *Art Journal* (New York) 40, no. 4 (Fall–Winter 1980): 375.

———. "Post-TV Art." *Portfolio* (New York), July–August 1982: 76–79.

———. "Robert Longo's Solid Vision." *New York Beat*, 2 May 1984: 8–9.

Golden, Deven. "A Review of Longo at Donald Young Gallery." *New Art Examiner* (Chicago) 14, no. 4 (December 1986): 42–43.

Groot, Paul. "Alchemy and the Rediscovery of the Human Figure in Recent Art." *Flash Art* (Milan), no. 126 (February–March 1986): 42–43.

Hatton, B. "Urban Kisses: New York at the ICA." *Artscribe* (London), no. 38 (December 1982): 16–21.

Henry, Gerrit. "Pictures." *Artnews* (New York) 77, no. 1 (January 1978): 142–43.

Hicks, Emily. "Death in the Age of Mechanical Reproduction." *Artweek* (Oakland, California), 4 July 1981.

Hill, A. "Being Bad." *Artscribe* (London), no. 32 (December 1981): 17.

Howell, John. "Reviews: Robert Longo, The Brooklyn Museum." *Artforum* (New York) 24, no. 2 (October 1985): 120–21.

Hughes, Robert. "Careerism and Hype amidst the Image Haze." *Time* (New York), 17 June 1985: 78–83.

———. "Lost among the Figures." *Time* (New York), 31 May 1982: 64–67.

———. "Three from the Image Machine.' *Time* (New York), 14 March 1983: 83–84.

Huntington, Richard. "The Good, the Bad, and the Ugly."*Artnews* (New York) 87, no.1 (January 1988): 9.

Hutton, Jon. "The Anxious Figure." *Arts Magazine* (New York) 56, no. 5 (January 1982): 17.

James, D. E. "Sculpture of Death." *Artweek* (Oakland, California), 5 January 1985.

Jarmusch, Ann. "Image Scavengers." *Artnews* (New York) 82, no. 3 (March 1983): 111.

Jones, Alan. "Robert Longo Goes to Hollywood." *New York Talk Magazine*, May 1986: 34–39.

Kalil, Susie. "Issues in Extension: Contemporary Arts Museums." *Artweek* (Oakland, California), 9 February 1980.

Knight, Christopher. "Realism with a Human Face." *Los Angeles Herald Examiner*, 24 June 1981.

Kontova, Helena. "From Performance to Painting." *Flash Art* (Milan), no. 106 (February–March 1982): 16–20.

Kulenkampff, Verena. "In der Sprache der Gewalt." *Art/Das Kunstmagazin* (Hamburg), September 1985: 76–85.

Kuspit, Donald B. " 'New Figuration in America' at the Milwaukee Art Museum." *Art in America* (New York) 71, no. 9 (September 1983): 178–79.

———. "Robert Longo: Metro Pictures." *Artforum* (New York) 25, no. 6 (February 1987): 111.

Larson, Kay. "Into the Light." *New York Magazine,* 17 November 1986: 93–94.

———. "Sculpting Figuratively." *New York Magazine,* 16 November 1981: 120–23.

Lawson, Thomas. " 'Pictures' at Artists Space." *Art in America* (New York) 55, no. 1 (January–February 1978): 118.

———. "Switching Channels." *Flash Art* (Milan), no. 102 (March–April 1981): 21.

———. "The Uses of Representation: Making Some Distinctions." *Flash Art* (Milan), no. 88–89 (March–April 1979): 37–39.

Levin, Kim. "New York: Robert Longo, Metro Pictures." *Flash Art* (Milan), no. 102 (March–April 1981): 40.

Lewis, Christopher. "Mondo Longo." *Art in America* (New York) 77, no. 3 (March 1989): 35–39.

Lifson, Ben. "La Photographie de la forme au contenu." *Art Press* (Paris), no. 108 (November 1986): 25–29.

Lippard, Lucy R. "Cross-Country Music." *The Village Voice* (New York), 8 March 1983.

McGill, Douglas C. "Art People." *The New York Times*, 31 October 1986.

———. "Art People: Robert Longo and Collaborators." *The New York Times*, 30 May 1986.

McLellan, Joseph. "Enigmatic Empire." *The Washington Post,* 16 April 1981.

Madoff, S. H. "What Is Postmodern about Painting: The Scandinavia Lectures II." *Arts Magazine* (New York) 60, no. 2 (October 1985): 59–64.

Mahoney, J. W. "Robert Longo: Metro Pictures." *New Art Examiner* (Chicago) 14, no. 6 (February 1987): 57.

Marmer, Nancy. "Isms on the Rhine." *Art in America* (New York) 69, no. 11 (November 1981): 116.

Marzorati, Gerald. "Monumental Confrontations." *Soho Weekly News* (New York), 8 April 1981.

———. "Your Show of Shows." *Artnews* (New York) 83, no. 11 (September 1984): 62–65.

Melville, Stephen. "Notes on the Reemergence of Allegory, the Forgetting of Modernism, the Necessity of Rhetoric, and the Conditions of Publicity in Art Criticism." *October* (New York), no. 19 (Winter 1981): 55–92.

Messerli, Douglas. "Robert Longo: Empire." *Artxpress* (Providence, Rhode Island) 1, no. 3 (September–October 1981): 58.

Millet, Catherine. "L'Ingratitude de l'art." *Art Press* (Paris), no. 85 (October 1984): 4–12.

Morris, Gay. "Longo Proves He Is 'Major.' " *Peninsula Times Tribune* (Palo Alto, California), 24 May 1984.

Moore, John M. "Return of the Emotive." *Connaissance des Arts* (Paris), no. 26 (March 1982): 54–61.

Morris, Robert. "American Quartet." *Art in America* (New York) 69, no. 12 (December 1981): 92–105.

Moser, Charlotte. "Renaissance Show Surveys 10 Years of Using Human Forms in Sculpture." *Chicago Sun-Times*, 29 May 1983.

Muchnic, Suzanne. "Constant Lure of Longo's 'Men.' " *Los Angeles Times,* 31 March 1986.

———. "Is L.A. Ready for a 'Crash' Course in Longo's Art." *Los Angeles Times,* 8 November 1984.

Mueller, Cookie. "Larger than Life: The World of Robert Longo." *Saturday Review* (New York), November–December 1985: 44–48, 90.

Nechvatal, Joseph. "Post Simulation Decadence." *Arts Magazine* (New York) 61, no. 10 (Summer 1987): 28–29.

Nilson, Lisbet. "Making It Neo." *Artnews* (New York) 82, no. 7 (September 1983): 62–70.

Oille, Jennifer. "Stock Exchange Art." *Canadian Forum* (Toronto), August–September 1983: 46–47.

Olander, William. "Art and Politics of Arms and the Artist." *Art in America* (New York) 73, no. 6 (June 1985): 59–63.

Onorato, Ronald J. "Desperados and Madonnas: Italian Art Today." *Artxpress* (Providence, Rhode Island) 2, no. 1 (January–February 1982): 20–24.

———. "Tableaus, Wave Hill." *Artxpress* (Providence, Rhode Island) 1, no. 6 (November–December 1981): 62–63.

Ostrow, Joanne. "Performance Art: Is It Art, or Theater, or Just a Put-on?" *The Washington Post,* 10 April 1981.

Owens, Craig. "The Allegorical Impulse: Toward a Theory of Postmodernism, Part 1." *October* (New York), no. 12 (Spring 1980): 67–86.

———. "The Allegorical Impulse: Toward a Theory of Postmodernism, Part 2." *October* (New York), no. 13 (Summer 1980): 58–80.

———. "Robert Longo at Metro Pictures." *Art in America* (New York) 56, no. 3 (March 1981): 125–26.

Padgham, Gay. "New York Highlights." *London Morning Star.* 22 November 1982.

Perron, Wendy. "On the Rocks." *Soho Weekly News* (New York), 4 May 1978.

Phillips, Lisa. " 'High' Art: The Thrill of Pain Caused by Modern Art Is Like an Addiction." *Art and Text* 22 (1986): 19–26.

Pincus-Witten, Robert. "Defenestrations: Robert Longo and Ross Bleckner." *Arts Magazine* (New York) 57, no. 3 (November 1982): 94–95.

———. "Entries: Propaedeutica." *Arts Magazine* (New York) 58, no. 7 (March 1984): 94–96.

———. "Entries: Sheer Grunge." *Arts Magazine* (New York) 55, no. 9 (May 1981): 93–97.

Plous, Phyllis. "Heritage Renewed: Representational Drawing Today." *American Artist* (New York) 47 (July 1983): 66–71, 88–89.

Prager, Emily. "Mondo Longo." *Interview* (New York), May 1988: 87–89.

Ratcliff, Carter. "Biennial Grievances." *Saturday Review* (New York), May–June 1983: 39–40.

———. "Contemporary American Art." *Flash Art* (Milan), no. 108 (Summer 1982): 32–35.

———. "Dali's Dreadful Relevance." *Artforum* (New York) 20, no. 2 (October 1982): 64.

———. "The Distractions of Theme." *Art in America* (New York) 69, no. 11 (November 1981): 19, 21, 23.

———. "Hot Young Artists, Art Stars for the Eighties." *Saturday Review* (New York), 8 February 1981: 12–15, 20.

———. "Robert Longo." *Interview* (New York), April 1983: 78–81.

———. "Robert Longo: Les Méchanismes ambigus de l'image d'image." *Art Press* (Paris), no. 100 (February 1986): 12–15.

———. "Robert Longo Survival Art: Urban Prophet." *Elle* (New York), October 1986: 86–88.

———. "Robert Longo: The City of Sheer Image." *Print Collector's Newsletter* (New York) 14 (July–August 1983): 95–98.

———. "Westkunst: Robert Longo." *Flash Art* (Milan), no. 103 (Summer 1981): 30–31.

Rickey, Carrie. "Naive Nouveau and Its Malcontents." *Flash Art* (Milan), no. 98–99 (Summer 1980): 39.

Rimanelli, David. "Robert Longo, Metro Pictures." *Artforum* (New York) 26, no. 5 (January 1989): 110–11.

"Robert Longo: The Painted 'Moving' Picture." *Mizue* (Tokyo), Spring 1989.

Roberts, John. "The Art of Self-Attention." *Artscribe* (London), no. 36 (August 1982): 50–55.

———. "Masks and Mirrors." *Art Monthly* (London), February 1983: 5–9.

Rose, Barbara. "Art in Discoland." *Vogue* (New York), September 1985: 668–72, 747.

Schwartz, Ellen. "Artists the Critics Are Watching: Robert Longo. 'Art Is Like a Fall Downstairs.' " *Artnews* (New York) 80, no. 5 (May 1981): 82–83.

Shore, Michael. "Punk Rocks the Art World." *Artnews* (New York) 79, no. 9 (November 1980): 78–85.

Siegel, Jeanne. "Figuratively Sculpting." *Artxpress* (Providence, Rhode Island) 2, no. 2 (March–April 1982): 64.

———. "Lois Lane and Robert Longo: Interpretation of Image." *Arts Magazine* (New York) 55, no. 3 (November 1980): 154–57.

———. "The New Reliefs." *Arts Magazine* (New York) 56, no. 8 (April 1982): 140–44.

Silverthorne, Jeanne. " 'Tableaux' Wave Hill." *Artforum* (New York) 20, no. 3 (November 1981): 85–86.

Simon, Joan. "Double Takes." *Art in America* (New York) 68, no. 10 (October 1980): 115.

Small, Michael. "Already a Big Man on Canvas, Robert Longo Goes Multimedia." *People* (New York), 10 November 1986: 135–36.

Smith, Roberta. "Appropriation über Alles." *The Village Voice* (New York), 11 January 1983.

———. "Material Concerns." *The Village Voice* (New York), 29 May 1984.

———. "Mocking Impressions." *The Village Voice* (New York), 1 March 1983.

———. "Robert Longo." *The New York Times*, 4 November, 1988.

Staebler, Wendy. "Enlightened Design." *Interiors* (New York) 46 (November 1986): 138.

Storr, Robert. "L'Aclatement de l'école de New York." *Art Press* (Paris), no. 100 (February 1986): 46–48.

Sturman, John. "Robert Longo, Metro Pictures." *Artnews* (New York) 88, no. 1 (January 1989): 132.

Tatransky, Valentin. "Pictures." *Arts Magazine* (New York) 52, no. 4 (December 1977): 17.

Tennant, Donna. "Four Artists Struggle for Originality." *Houston Chronicle,* 27 January 1980.

Upshaw, Reagan. "Figuratively Sculpting at P.S. 1." *Art in America* (New York) 70, no. 3 (March 1982): 143.

Venant, Elizabeth. "Current Wonders of the Art World: Neo-Expressionism." *The Los Angeles Times,* 28 April 1985.

———. "Robert Longo: A Fix on Junk Culture." *The Los Angeles Times,* 28 April 1985, Calendar.

Wallis, Brian. "Governing Authority: Robert Longo's Performance 'Empire.' " *Wedge* (New York) 1 (Summer 1982): 64–71.

Weisberg, Ruth. "Representational Drawing." *Art-week* (Oakland, California), 2 April 1983.

Welzenbach, Michael. "The Ups and Downs of Stardom: An Interview with Robert Longo." *New Art Examiner* (Chicago) 11, no. 4 (December 1984): 41–43.

Wiedmann, Christopher. "Tanz auf dem Vulkan: Arbeiten von Robert Longo in München." *Suddeutsche Zeitung* (Munich), 9 June 1983.

Wilson, Judith. "Outside Chances." *The Village Voice* (New York), 8 July 1981.

Wilson, William. "Larry Gagosian: Robert Longo Exhibit." *The Los Angeles Times,* 26 June 1981.

Zelevansky, Lynn. "Documenta: Art for Art's Sake." *Flash Art* (Milan), no. 109 (November 1982): 39–40.

———. "New York Reviews." *Artnews* (New York) 82, no. 8 (April 1983): 152.

Zimmer, William. "Art Goes to Rock World on Fire." *Soho Weekly News* (New York), 27 September 1979.

———. "Flash Art Reviews." *Flash Art* (Milan), no. 112 (May 1983): 60–61.

———. "Robert Longo." *Soho Weekly News* (New York), 21 January 1981.

———. "Where Buffalo Roams." *Soho Weekly News* (New York), 16 July 1980.

Checklist of the Exhibition

National Trust, 1981
Charcoal and graphite on paper; cast aluminum
Three panels, overall 63 × 234 in. (310 × 594 cm)
Walker Art Center, Minneapolis
Art Center Acquisition Fund, 1981
Pages 84–85

Untitled, 1981
Charcoal and graphite on paper
96 × 60 in. (244 × 152 cm)
Collection Phoebe Chason, New York
Page 76

Untitled, 1981
Charcoal and graphite on paper
96 × 60 in. (244 × 152 cm)
Collection Metro Pictures, New York
Page 74

Untitled, 1981
Charcoal and graphite on paper
96 × 60 in. (244 × 152 cm)
Collection Metro Pictures, New York
Page 73

Untitled, 1981
Charcoal and graphite on paper
96 × 48 in. (244 × 122 cm)
Collection Arthur and Carol Goldberg, New York
Page 78

Untitled, 1981
Charcoal, graphite, ink, and tempera on paper
96 × 60 in. (244 × 152 cm)
Collection B. Z. and Michael Schwartz, New York
Page 83

Untitled, 1981
Charcoal and graphite on paper
96 × 60 in. (244 × 152 cm)
PaineWebber Group, Inc., New York
Page 77

Corporate Wars: Walls of Influence, 1982
Lacquer on wood and steel; cast aluminum
Three panels, overall 108 × 302 × 48 in. (274 × 768 × 122 cm)
The Saatchi Collection, London
Pages 30, 86–87

Untitled, 1982
Charcoal and graphite on paper
96 × 48 in. (244 × 122 cm)
Collection Mr. and Mrs. Robert K. Hoffman, Dallas
Page 78

Untitled, 1982
Charcoal and graphite on paper
96 × 48 in. (244 × 122 cm)

Collection Gerald S. Elliott, Chicago
Page 79

Culture Culture, 1982–83
Acrylic on Masonite; charcoal, graphite, oil, acrylic, and ink on paper with plexiglass
Two panels, overall 91½ × 147¾ in. (232.5 × 375 cm)
Collection the artist
Pages 51, 90

Master Jazz, 1982–83
Lacquer on wood; charcoal, graphite, and ink on paper; silkscreen and acrylic on Masonite
Four panels, overall 96 × 225 × 12 in. (244 × 571.5 × 30.5 cm)
The Menil Collection, Houston
Pages 92–93

Pressure, 1982–83
Lacquer on wood; charcoal, graphite, and ink on paper
Two panels, overall 101½ × 90 × 37¾ in. (258 × 229 × 96 cm)
The Museum of Modern Art, New York
Gift of the Louis and Bessie Adler Foundation,
Seymour M. Klein, President, New York
Pages 33, 91

Untitled, 1982–84
Charcoal, graphite, and dye on paper
96 × 60 in. (244 × 152 cm)
Collection the artist
Page 75

Now Everybody (for R. W. Fassbinder), II. 1982–89
Charcoal, graphite, and ink on paper; cast bronze
Four panels, overall 96 × 192 in. (244 × 488 cm);
bronze, 79 × 28 × 45 in. (200 × 71 × 114 cm)
Collection the artist
Not illustrated; see first version, pages 88–89

Black Palms, 1983
Lacquer, acrylic, and metal on wood
120 × 96 × 29½ in. (305 × 244 × 75 cm)
Collection Mr. and Mrs. C. Bagley Wright, Seattle
Page 38, 98

Ornamental Love, 1983
Oil, metal, and linoleum on wood; charcoal, graphite, and ink on paper; cast bronze
Three panels, overall 101½ × 202 × 18 in. (258 × 513 × 46 cm)
Collection Janet Green, London
Pages 94–95

Sword of the Pig, 1983
Lacquer on wood; charcoal and graphite on paper; plexiglass; silkscreen on aluminum plate
Three panels, overall 97¾ × 229½ × 28 in. (248 × 582 × 71 cm)

Tate Gallery, London
Pages 96–97

We Want God, 1983–84
Marble; wood; oil on aluminum
Three panels, overall 96 × 115 in. (244 × 292 cm)
Collection Eugene and Barbara Schwartz, New York
Page 99

Tongue to the Heart, 1984
Acrylic and oil on wood; cast plaster; hammered lead on wood; Durotran; acrylic, charcoal, and graphite on canvas
Four panels, overall 136 × 216 × 25 in. (345 × 549 × 63 cm)
The Saatchi Collection, London
Pages 100–101

All You Zombies: Truth before God, 1986
Acrylic and charcoal on shaped canvas; cast bronze on motorized platform of steel and wood
Overall, 176½ × 195 × 177½ in. (448 × 495.3 × 451 cm)
Collection the artist
Pages 43, 108–109

Death and Taxes, 1986
Wood, Cor-ten steel, dollar bills, and acrylic on wood
Overall, 96 × 92 × 36 in. (244 × 234 × 91 cm)
The Art Institute of Chicago
Restricted gift of Eli Broad Family Foundation, Mrs. Sandra Crown, Mr. and Mrs. Thomas Dittmer, Gerald S. Elliott, David Meitus in memory of A. James Speyer, Joseph R. Shapiro, Allen Turner, Kate L. Brewster Fund, Estate of Louis Lasker Fund, Mrs. Clive Runnels Fund, and the Goodman Fund
Page 115

In Civil War, 1986
Silkscreen on canvas, wood, steel
92¼ × 93 × 5 in. (235 × 236 × 13 cm)
Collection Metro Pictures, New York
Page 103

Lenny Bleeds: Comet in a Bomber, 1986
Acrylic, oil, diamond dust, graphite, and carbon on canvas; Durotran; steel; aluminum; and cast bronze
118 × 378 × 39 in. (300 × 960 × 100 cm)
Collection the Eli Broad Family Foundation, Los Angeles
Pages 106–107

Machines in Love, 1986
Silkscreen and enamel on aluminum; acrylic and oil on wood
Overall, 146 × 133 × 63½ in. (371 × 338 × 161 cm)
Collection Ichizo Ichimura, Osaka, Japan
Pages 2, 113

Now Is a Creature: The Fly, 1986
Acrylic, charcoal, and graphite on canvas; steel
82 × 140 × 26 in. (208 × 355 × 66 cm)
Collection Gerald S. Elliott, Chicago
Page 104

End of the Season, 1987
Linoleum on wood; enamel on steel; chromeplated cast bronze
96 × 96 × 18 in. (244 × 244 × 45.8 cm)
Daniel Templon Foundation, Paris
Page 114

Black Planet (for A.Z.), 1988
Oil paint on steel; Neoprene
110 × 110 × 72 in. (279 × 279 × 183 cm)
Collection the artist
Page 125

Dumb Running: The Theory of the Brake, 1988
Gold leaf on steel, mounted on recessed steel support, with motor and timer
73 × 126 × 18¾ in. (185 × 320 × 47 cm)
The Langer Collection, New York
Pages 46, 116

The Fire Next Time (for G.B.), 1988
Graphite on cast aluminum and fiberglass; aluminum; plexiglass
74½ × 210½ × 12½ in. (189 × 534 × 32 cm)
The Rivendell Collection
Page 122

A House Divided: Re-enactor, 1988
Wool felt on aluminum; stainless steel; acrylic paint on aluminum
88 × 126 × 6½ in. (224 × 295 × 16 cm)
Courtesy Metro Pictures, New York
Page 120

Hum: Making Ourselves, 1988
Formica, plastic tubing, audio jacks, chromeplated steel, aluminum, plastic bonding, and lacquer on wood and steel
Two parts, top: 63¾ × 125⅝ × 5⅜ in. (162 × 319 × 13.7 cm); bottom: 24 × 125⅝ × 28 in. (61 × 319 × 71 cm); overall 90¾ × 125⅝ × 28 in. (230.5 × 319 × 71 cm)
Collection Barbara and Richard Lane, New York
Page 121

Joker: Force of Choice, 1988
Cor-ten steel
Four parts, overall 112½ × 115½ × 18½ in. (286 × 293 × 45.7 cm)
Collection the artist
Page 117

ACKNOWLEDGMENTS

One of the most pleasurable aspects of producing an exhibition catalogue such as this is the opportunity it affords to thank the many colleagues and associates, old and new, who have taken part in the gestation of the exhibition over the course of a year and a half. I am extremely grateful to the sizable ensemble of talented individuals who have contributed to the realization of this project. Not everyone can be mentioned here, but to all who participated in this enterprise, I extend the same gratitude as I do to those singled out here for their especially notable contributions in bringing this presentation to life.

My first thanks, of course, go to Director Earl A. Powell III for his early and steadfast support of this ambitious undertaking, long before there was a sponsor to enable it to come to fruition. I thank him too for his loyalty during the exhibition's long and sometimes complicated development.

Within the Museum, many colleagues were called upon to meet the challenge of assembling, transporting, installing, and caring for the works in this presentation. I am pleased to thank Elizabeth Algermissen, Assistant Director, Exhibitions and Programs, and John Passi, Head, Exhibition Programs, for attending so thoughtfully to all the usual, and some not-so-usual, institutional requisites. I extend my special thanks to Arthur Owens, Acting Assistant Director, Operations, who oversaw, with characteristic adroitness, the formidable task of coordinating activities throughout the Museum to stage this exceptionally robust show. Registrar Renee Montgomery and her able staff arranged for the packing and shipment of the works—many of which are large and unwieldy—and I thank them, as I do Pieter Meyers, Head of Conservation, Steven Cristin-Poucher, Objects Conservator, and Victoria Blyth-Hill, Paper Conservator, for ensuring that the works were in proper condition before, during, and after their display in Los Angeles and elsewhere. Independent designer Brent Saville's imposing design for the exhibition galleries is carefully attuned to the spirit of Robert Longo's works. And it is my special pleasure to thank my secretary Wendy Owen for her indefatigable efforts toward the realization of every part of this project; she is a valued colleague and a deft team player.

This complex project has also benefitted from the ever-reliable efforts of Jennifer Cox and Nicholas Arbatsky, Robert Longo's studio assistants, and Victoria Hamburg, his video and film producer. Helene Winer and Janelle Reiring, the artist's gallery representatives at Metro Pictures in New York, and their assistant, David Goldsmith, have been endlessly helpful in providing essential primary information, photographs, and a virtual cache of other materials on Robert Longo and his works, and I thank them all heartily.

This catalogue, for many of its readers, is likely to be their only experience of the exhibition, and therefore tantamount to it. The skills and dedication of numerous individuals have been brought to bear in its creation. I am most grateful to Hal Foster, Katherine Dieckmann, and Brian Wallis for their invaluable contributions; the range of their well-expressed viewpoints enriches this volume. In the Museum, Managing Editor Mitch Tuchman facilitated our copublication of this catalogue with Rizzoli International Publications; I thank him for his support and advocacy. Museum intern Linda Samuels and the department's able and esteemed volunteer Roz Leader pioneered the earliest version of the comprehensive bibliography and exhibition history that appear here. Graphic designer Steven Schoenfelder conceived this

201

book's poised and thoughtful design. At Rizzoli, Associate Editor Sarah Burns was resourceful and astute in conferring unity and composure to an anthology of contributions by the various authors, for which she has merited our collective thanks. Furthermore she has worked with Robert Longo in compiling the chronology and in bringing together the many illustrations that appear there and in the essays. And I extend warmest personal thanks to Senior Editor Jane Fluegel, who has become my good telephonic friend, for her careful supervision of every aspect of producing this book and for having as much good will as she has patience, and more patience than is probably good for an editor to have.

Without the generous and enthusiastic endorsement of this exhibition by the many private and institutional lenders, there could be no exhibition. On behalf of the Museum and the artist, I thank them one and all. And it is our proud pleasure to thank the Museum of Contemporary Art in Chicago and the Wadsworth Atheneum in Hartford, Connecticut, for their participation in hosting the exhibition's tour.

AT&T has been the enlightened corporate sponsor of several major programs at this Museum, and we are indebted to R. Z. Manna, Director of Corporate Underwriting and Arts Sponsorships, and his colleagues for making this exhibition possible, as well as for their support of a related program of performances at the UCLA Center for the Performing Arts.

And finally I must thank Robert Longo, whose extraordinary art and fast friendship I have treasured over a period of more than ten years. I have found him always to be as good a friend as he is an artist, and I am proud and gratified to have spent an important part of my professional and personal life in organizing this exhibition, which documents his remarkable achievement.

H.N.F.

FROM THE ARTIST:

Over the years I have had the pleasure of working with many collaborators, fabricators, and assistants—from experienced craftsmen to student interns—who have been of enormous help in the realization of my work. I would like to take this opportunity to thank them not only for their technical assistance but also for their friendship and for putting up with the incredible chaos I can sometimes create within the studio.

I would especially like to thank Nicholas Arbatsky, Edward Batcheller, Brand X, Peter Coates, Jennifer Cox, Joseph Di Monda, Rick Franklin, Victoria Hamburg, Mark Innerst, Dakota Jackson, Douglas Kolk, Steve Kovisto, Anna Kustera, Roger Longo, Kevin Noble, Frank Ockenfels, Ranieri Sculpture Casting, Maurice Sanchez, Jim Schmidt, Diane Shea, Jim Sheppard, Michael Sol-Morris, Tallix, and Cliff Wang.

In addition, I would like to thank those without whom this catalogue and the exhibition would not have been possible. I feel that the realization of both is the culmination of my ten-year friendship with Howard Fox, who was among the first to have written about my work. His assistant, Wendy Owen, has been particularly helpful in the organization of the exhibition, and Sarah Burns, our editor at Rizzoli, has been as important to publishing the catalogue. I value the friendship of Helene Winer and Janelle Reiring, of Metro Pictures, who have been supportive of my work from the very beginning. Finally, I want to thank my family and friends, especially Gretchen Bender. They have been a source of strength and inspiration to me.

R.L.

LENDERS TO THE EXHIBITION

Albright-Knox Art Gallery, Buffalo, New York
Brooke and Carolyn Alexander, New York
Alyssa Rabach Anthone and Kenneth D. Anthone,
Buffalo, New York
The Art Institute of Chicago
Maxine and Richard Brandenburg, Burlington, Vermont
The Eli Broad Family Foundation, Los Angeles
Phoebe Chason, New York
Gerald S. Elliott, Chicago
Arthur and Carol Goldberg, New York
Janet Green, London
Mr. and Mrs. Robert K. Hoffman, Dallas
Jane Holzer, New York
Ichizo Ichimura, Osaka, Japan
Marshall and Wallis Katz, Pittsburgh
Kasper König, Frankfurt, West Germany
Barbara and Richard Lane, New York

The Langer Collection, New York
Barbara and Oscar Leidenfrost, Los Angeles
Robert Longo, New York
The Menil Collection, Houston
Metro Pictures, New York
The Museum of Modern Art, New York
PaineWebber Group, Inc., New York
The Rivendell Collection
Fredrik Roos, Zug, Switzerland
The Saatchi Collection, London
B. Z. and Michael Schwartz, New York
Eugene and Barbara Schwartz, New York
Tate Gallery, London
Daniel Templon Foundation, Paris
Walker Art Center, Minneapolis
Helene Winer, New York
Mr. and Mrs. C. Bagley Wright, Seattle

205

ABOUT THE AUTHORS

Howard N. Fox, who organized the exhibition *Robert Longo,* is curator of contemporary art at the Los Angeles County Museum of Art. He is the author of "Desire for Pathos: The Art of Robert Longo," published in the journal *Sun and Moon* (1979), as well as *Avant-Garde in the Eighties* (1987).

Hal Foster, a critic of contemporary art and culture, is editor of the anthology *The Anti-Aesthetic: Essays on Postmodern Culture* (1983) and author of *Recodings: Art, Spectacle, Cultural Politics* (1985).

Katherine Dieckmann is a contributor to *The Village Voice* and has directed several music videos.

Brian Wallis, a senior editor of the magazine *Art in America,* assembled the anthology *Art after Modernism: Rethinking Representation* (1984).

PHOTOGRAPH CREDITS

A ROBERT LONGO.   23/6/87.

VUE DE DOS.

LA VUE DE JADIS M'A OUVERT LA VOIE
D'UN REPAIRE SANS IDÉE , SANS SOUCIS
OU TOUT DEMEURE EN L'ÉTAT.

L'ÉTAT DE CE LIEU IMÉDIT
N'INSCRIT AUCUNE AUTRE LOI
QUE CELLE DU DEVENIR.

L'ÉTÉ SEREIN DECRIT DEJA LE JOUR
OU LA VIE SERA ASSEZ GRANDE
POUR CONTENIR LA NUIT.

SILENCE, SECRET TOURMENT, STUPEUR.

PAUL VIRILIO.

TO ROBERT LONGO

SEEN FROM THE BACK

The vision of the past has given me the way
To a shelter without ideas, without worries
Where everything dwells in its own state.

The state of this new place
Records no other law
Than that of becoming.

The calm summer describes the day
Where life will be large enough
To consume the night.

Silence, secret torture, stupor.